WAR TIME, PEACE TIME, MY TIME

WAR TIME, PEACE TIME, MY TIME

DORICE GREENFIELD

BLOOMSBURY READER
LONDON · OXFORD · NEW YORK · NEW DELHI · SYDNEY

This edition published in 2015 by Bloomsbury Reader

Copyright © 2015 Dorice Greenfield

The moral right of the author is asserted.

Bloomsbury Reader is an imprint of Bloomsbury Publishing Plc

50 Bedford Square, London WC1B 3DP

www.bloomsburyreader.com

Bloomsbury is a trademark of Bloomsbury Publishing plc

Bloomsbury Publishing, London, Oxford, New Delhi, New York and Sydney

ISBN: 978 1 4482 1567 6
eISBN: 978 1 4482 1566 9

Visit www.bloomsburyreader.com to find out more about our authors and their books.
You will find extracts, author interviews, author events and you can sign up for
newsletters to be the first to hear about our latest releases and special offers.

You can also find us on Twitter @bloomsreader.

Printed and bound by CPI Group (UK) Ltd, Croydon, CR0 4YY

For Reg, Susan and Graham

Contents

Introduction   1

Preface   4

Prologue   6

Chapter 1: The Early Years: 1927–1938   8

Chapter 2: Secondary School Days: 1938–1941   27

Chapter 3: The Dancing Years: 1941–1947   39

Chapter 4: The War Years: 1939–1945   54

Chapter 5: The Love of My Life: 1941–1950   67

Chapter 6: Settling Down: 1950–2005   80

Chapter 7: The End of an Era: 2005–2010   94

Chapter 8: 'Till Death Do Us Part': 2011–2012   103

Chapter 9: New Beginnings: Dancing Again: 2012–   107

Epilogue   113

Photographs   115

A Note on the Author   125

Introduction

Our Mum's life has been simultaneously ordinary and extraordinary: but if the following pages are anything to go by, she doesn't seem to be aware of any such distinction.

Mum was born in 1927 into a typical working class English family, the youngest of three children and the only girl. As was normal in those days, she left school aged fourteen, got a job, married in her early twenties and had two kids. Now a widow coming up to eighty-eight, she's in amazing physical and mental health and lives comfortably in sheltered accommodation. So why would you want to read her story?

Look more closely and you'll see that her seemingly humdrum existence has brushed against the tectonic plates of culture, class and religion that clashed across the mid-20th century. Mum chose active engagement rather than a ringside seat. As a scholarship kid from a poor home, with cardboard soles on her shoes, she fetched up at one of the best independent girls' schools in the country. She's always stood up for herself: against snobs, against prejudice about being on the stage, against intolerance towards those who married a Jew in an age of rampant anti-Semitism. Because she chose to make the difficult but correct decisions rather than the easy, wrong ones, I hope her story will be inspirational to anyone struggling with comparable socio-economic challenges some sixty to seventy years later.

But it's at the personal level that this brief book is compelling. Coping with the indignity of the loos in air-raid shelters, improvising hair-dye and make-up and dancing in shows despite the bombs falling outside – these are all remembered positively. Her schemes included saving up money so she could run away from school without telling anyone and, later in wartime, so she could snatch a few hours at The Palais before her dancing partners left for the war – some of them inevitably to be killed.

Courage and love run as consistent themes throughout her story. The bond she had with Dad provided the strongest of backgrounds for my brother and me to grow up confident and secure. We never had spare money – unflagging encouragement was so much more valuable.

When we were children, I took our family values for granted: I thought everyone saw the funny and bright side of life and was honest. Mum used to say, 'I'd rather have a thief than a liar': she operated a penal discount scheme whereby if my brother or I fessed up to some misdemeanour, punishment would be reduced or waived, because 'you've owned up'. She also taught us to be ourselves: once when I was going to a teenage party where, for the first time, boys were going to be present, I was worried what they'd think of me. Mum's solution: 'You should worry instead what you think of them.' Or a little earlier when all my primary school friends were being bribed with offers of, say, a bicycle for passing the eleven plus, I had the simple deal of nothing whatsoever because 'If you pass, it must be because you want to and can, and if you don't, we'll still love you'. And right back at the beginning when I was born, I think her dream was that I'd take over where she'd had to leave off when she got married, by being a professional dancer – I was dispatched to ballet classes pretty much as soon as I could walk. But as soon as she realised I was a bookworm, my dreams became her dreams. It's so typical of Mum that none of this brilliant parenting is recorded in her book, probably because it all came too naturally to seem of note to her.

When I was a toddler, if people we met in the street asked how old I was, Mum would reply. 'Ask her – let her speak for herself'. So here's my very ordinary but extraordinary Mum speaking for herself.

Susan Greenfield
Oxford, July 2015

Preface

You could be wondering why an old lady suddenly writes a book. As it is a funny sort of reason, I thought you might like to know.

I was coming out of Age Concern when I noticed a magazine called Bookbite on the table. The lady in charge gave me permission to take it home, and as I glanced through it I saw it was full of short stories. After my lunch I sat down to read one of these stories when a leaflet fell out. On picking it up I saw it was a competition called 'Write a letter to yourself in 500 words'. This sounded fun, I thought; why not have a go?

It took me a couple of days to write my story, which I called 'Miracles do Happen'. My brother read it and turned up his nose, but my daughter seemed amused and asked about the closing date. Like an idiot I had not thought of that. Oh dear! The deadline was 2010, two years previously, so that was the end of that. Or so I thought.

Shortly afterwards, *The Times* newspaper wanted me for a photoshoot in Oxford with my daughter for Mother's Day, and I was being taken there by the journalist Sue Fox. On the way I told her about the competition and she asked me to show her my effort. Much to my surprise she liked it and told me to send it off anyway. After talking to my family and taking a lot of teasing, I sent off my little letter, never expecting a reply. Then a couple of weeks later I actually did hear from Anna Logan at *Bookbite*. She praised my story and said it was book worthy, as well as sending me four lovely books to read.

Susan, my daughter, was very interested and said, 'Mum you must try to write a book, you have nothing to lose'. So I thought, why not?

Off to Smith's for writing paper, pens and everything I might need. I did not realise the task I had set myself. Oh yes I had my computer, but was still learning how to use it. Writing by hand at first then typing it into the computer with one finger was time consuming, but to send it to my friend was the problem. Emails – what are they? And attachments? Gosh, I will never cope. Time and trouble but at last I got the hang of it. My son and my sheltered scheme manager helped me with the computer and I started to enjoy writing. Remembering the past was fun; I had a little cry and a little laugh at some of my memories, still so clear in my head.

So I know now if I am asked to do something I have never done before I will have a shot at it, and say to myself, oh well, it will be a giggle if I can't but how super if I can and I will be so happy with myself for trying.

Prologue

It was 1932. I was five years old and so excited I could feel butterflies in my stomach. My mum was going to take me to a dancing class as I was so shy. She said, 'It will bring you out of yourself. I'm fed up with you hiding behind my skirts when I meet my friends in the street, or you running out into the garden if any visitors call.'

So we were standing in front of the dance teacher's house and I felt so nervous. Mum pulled me round the back of her and I peered out from behind, and when she rang the bell a beautiful lady answered the door. Mum asked about the dancing and the lady said, 'Would you like to come in and watch? We have a lesson in progress.'

The studio was very large with a big mirror on one wall and a long wooden bar opposite for practice. All along the bar were girls swinging their legs and some even had a leg right up on the bar, bending their head down to their knee. All the girls wore little black pleated skirts with white blouses which had a red 'M' on the pocket. This looked like fun to me!

We sat down on a long bench and the music started. The girls ran into a line and to me it was simply a wonderland. They jumped and kicked and danced and the beautiful lady, who I now knew was Miss Merlwyn, called out, 'Point your toes, girls!', 'Jean! Do not look at your feet' and 'Audrey, watch those arms and for goodness sake *smile*'. Then after a while, she called out, 'Yes, that's better, very nice, well done!'

Oh yes, Mum was right. I wanted to join in and start right away. Miss Merlwyn told Mum that it was fine and I could start next week. I could hardly wait. I was hooked and dancing became my love, my life, my world.

My story starts in 1927, with my poor but loving, working-class family life, and takes you with me all through the 1930s, the horrific war years and right up until today. Goodness, so much has changed. I want to share with you the times we laughed and sang, the times we wept and worried, my life as a dancer, a wife and a mother.

1

The Early Years
1927–1938

I was born on the sofa in our front room on 16 November 1927, in a lovely house in Southfield Road, Acton, in west London. There was no time to get my mum upstairs on the bed, but Nellie our neighbour was there to help. Now, dear Nellie was the kindest living soul, always cheerful, always ready to help out and if the midwife was late, she'd do the delivery. She knew what to do if a baby wouldn't feed, or if someone had a cough; no qualifications at all but everyone in the neighbourhood would call for Nellie if they had a problem. So when Mum went into labour, she sent for Nellie. As soon as Nellie arrived in her clean white pinny, I was already starting to enter this wonderful world. Nellie quickly put towels on the sofa and tied an old sheet round the leg of the sofa so Mum could pull on it when she felt the contractions. No gas and air in those days.

So it was, that without much fuss, I made my first public appearance.

When I was three, we moved to the downstairs flat of a corner house: 64 Rylett Crescent, Shepherd's Bush, and that's where I stayed until after my marriage in 1948.

The garden had a wall round it and Dad grew a hedge, which was his pride and joy. The small bedroom, where my two brothers slept in single iron beds, looked out onto this garden, as did the front room, which was kept for special occasions only. Opposite was the main bedroom, where my parents slept in a double bed, and I had a small bed in the corner.

Our kitchen window looked out onto a long wide garden path, which led up to the coal sheds and Dad's shed, with his barrow having pride of place by the gate. He managed to create two strips of garden for his runner beans and flowers on the edge at each path and by his barrow. Woozy, my cat, would sit up on the garden wall and if any dog passed he would jump on their backs and scare them.

The scullery door led to the garden and on the wall, high up, was the meat safe. No fridges or freezers in the 1930s. The meat safe was a wooden box with mesh sides to keep your meat in as it was cooler outside. We did the same for milk. My mother used to fill her large saucepan with water and leave the bottles overnight because milk came in glass bottles, not cartons or plastic like today, and would be delivered fresh every day to our doorstep.

When we first lived in the flat, the lavatory was outside, but as my dad was a master builder he was able to convert the larder in the kitchen into a small indoor lavatory. It was very basic compared with today, and even the toilet paper was different. We didn't have the luxury of soft paper – it was hard, smooth, thin white paper in rolls; the one Mum used to get was called San Izal. If Mum was broke, which was not uncommon, and the toilet roll ran out, Dad would cut newspaper into squares, make a hole in the corner, thread a piece of string through the holes then tie the string to form a loop so you had a pad of newspaper cuttings to use. I found if you tore a piece of the pad and rubbed it in your hands it would soften up, and of course it also gave you something to read whilst on the toilet. Not ideal, but better than nothing.

Friday night was bath night. Dad bought the zinc bath into the kitchen living room from outside and put it in front of the fire and the big kettles went on, to heat all the water to fill the bath. I was bathed first while Dad took the boys into the front room to read comics until it was their turn. The bath had been put near the fire and I enjoyed it very much. But after the bath was not so nice, as Mum gave us all cod liver oil, which I hated, and the laxative syrup of figs (even if you didn't need it). Then the boys had the same treatment, followed by cocoa and bed.

The front room was the best room, kept spotless and only used if we had company. There was a piano, a three-piece suite, a dining table and chairs, and Dad's desk. The fender around the fireplace had seats each end to sit on, with a highly polished brass poker and shovel and a small coal box. Mum was proud of this room and it was kept spick and span. When we had visitors, Mum would play the piano and Dad would lean on it and sing. Mum was self-taught but could knock out a tune by ear. Dad always sang 'Roll along Prairie Moon', and those types of song. It was good fun and sometimes Mum would let me show off and do a dance for our friends.

Dad had a cigarette machine in the house. When he wanted a packet of cigarettes he would put his money in the slot at the top and hey presto – a little drawer opened holding his cigarettes! The machine was like a little cupboard with a glass panel in the front so you could see when it was empty. The cigarette man came every Friday to take the money and fill it up. Sometimes Dad had 'borrowed' the money by putting a knife in the slot and somehow wriggling it to get some cash out. But he always put it back by Friday. He used to smoke Ardath or Player's cigarettes. They used to have cards in the boxes with all sorts of pictures: footballers, boxers, birds. My brother would collect these and swap them with friends to get a set.

My mother was frightened of thunderstorms and at the smallest rumble of thunder we were pushed into the cupboard under the stairs where the coats were kept, and warned not to come out until she said so. She used to open all doors to 'let the thunder bolt through'. I never quite worked out how a thunderbolt knew how to turn corners.

Every Monday Mum would do the washing in what we called the 'copper' – an ugly thing built into the wall with a fire underneath to heat the water. The wringer was in the garden and I used to turn the handle while Mum fed the washing between two rollers. It was then hung out to dry on a long washing line in the garden.

There was a local laundry service for what they called a 'bag wash'. This was a big white bag with a cord around the top to tie up which went in for a boil and cost eight pennies. Mum used to put sheets and towels in. It all came back spotless but of course not ironed. They had a proper laundry for ironing and starching but this was a more expensive service.

Our front door was almost as precious to my mum as the front room. The brass knocker and letter box were polished every day and you could really see your face in it. The step was cleaned every evening with Dad's whitewash so it was nice for the postman next morning.

When most people started having a red step, Mum dutifully followed and Dad painted ours red. It was washed and polished every day and most housewives used Cardinal polish, and the windows were cleaned with a drop of vinegar in water and polished with newspaper. Poor but posh!

Our streets were lit by gaslight and so was our home. You could see the gas man coming round on his bicycle and lighting the lamps as soon as it was dark, then in the morning he'd come round again and put them out.

In 1932, when I was about five, the electricians came and installed electricity into our home. It was like a new world – just flick a switch and it was so much brighter! There was a meter you put a shilling in and this would last for a couple of days. Mum was always shouting 'Is the light turned off?' when she heard you going out. About every three months the electric man came round and read the meter and he would usually give you a rebate of about four shillings. It was the same with the gas man but his meter took pennies so the rebate was far less. Mum looked forward to her rebates, especially if she was broke.

In the early days we had a crystal wireless set. This looked like a square box with a dial on the top and one set of headphones so we had to take turns to listen. It was not very satisfactory because you got a lot of whistle and interference.

When Dad got a proper wireless we couldn't believe it. We could all sit together and listen. His favourite programme was *In Town Tonight*, which started by giving you all the sounds from London at that time – noise of traffic, then a tram or a bus ticket conductor shouting, a newspaper man calling – then the programme would start. People were interviewed in the street so you would learn bits of news or hear reviews of new shows. It was a very entertaining programme and kept us up to date.

I first saw television in a shop window and couldn't believe it! There was what looked like a very big electric light bulb in a large cabinet with a lady talking. I rushed to Dad's work, as he was painting a shop window not far away, and he came back with me to see this wonderful invention. We didn't get our own TV, however, until about 1958 when someone gave us their old one.

There was a little grocery shop just around the corner from no. 64; it was run by a man called Mr Jones so we called the shop 'Jonesies'. Mum would send us to get a half penny worth of jam, which was a large tablespoon of jam put onto a piece of grease-proof paper then wrapped up. We would then say 'Please put it on Mum's bill' so he would check if she had paid her last bill and, if so, the jam would be handed over. Mum called this putting it 'on tick'. Mr Jones's little shop sold most things; you could have two slices of ham for a penny and this would be cut on a small machine with a big round cutting wheel, as he turned the handle. If you were lucky he would throw in little bits that had fallen off. This was real ham, much thicker and tastier than the plastic stuff we get today in packets.

Everything bought from the grocer was loose and sold in paper bags or wrapped in greaseproof paper. Sugar was weighed by the grocer then sold in a blue bag to the weight you wanted. Butter was in a massive block and a piece would be cut out and weighed. Then, with a pair of wooden paddles the size of table tennis bats, the grocer patted the butter into a rectangle, placed it on greaseproof paper, wrapped it up and gave it to you.

When Shredded Wheat first came out, it was a half penny for one portion, long before it came packaged in a box. I was hooked and eat it still today. We used to pop a knife in the end to split it in half and butter it inside then close it up. Ooh, it was delicious. Of course today most people eat it with milk.

Biscuits were in tins or boxes with a Bakelite see-through lid, which was used before plastic was invented, in front of the counter. You would point to which kind you wanted and the girl who was serving would come round and used a scoop to put the amount you wanted into a paper bag.

When you had finished shopping, you put it into your own basket or a brown paper bag with string handles – oh how those handles cut into your hands if the shopping was heavy! You were given the bill and then you went over to the cash desk to pay.

In some shops it was a little different. They put your money and the bill in a screw-top pot, pulled a handle and it whizzed over to the cashier's desk on a wire stretched across the ceiling. It then came back with your change in the same way, from the cashier's desk to the counter on another parallel wire.

You always paid cash or had it 'on tick'; no plastic cards like today, where you can buy what you really can't afford.

As a child if you couldn't afford it, you couldn't have it. Many's the time I've gone to school with cardboard in my shoes because they leaked water. If I had a hole in my sock I used to darn the hole with white cotton until Mum had a penny and three farthings for a new pair. Also, if the boys tore their trousers, a patch would be sewn in, not always with material that matched but Mum would try to get it as near as possible. Dad used to cut my hair but the boys would go to the barbers and have it cut fairly short for two pennies and they were given a small toffee bar. If I was with Mum waiting for them I would have my fingers crossed that the barber would give me a toffee bar as well.

Next door to the barbers was Cooke's pie and eel shop. When Mum could afford it, we would all go and have pie, mash and green liquor (parsley gravy), for four pennies a portion. This was a special treat for the four of us, as it would cost sixteen pennies,

14

and sometimes on the way home we would get a big bottle of Tizer, for two pennies.

This was fun because when we got home Mum would give my brother John the bottle, him being the eldest, and we would have a game of Stop and Go. You would shout 'Stop!' while he was drinking and he would stop and pass the bottle to Fred, again when you shouted 'Stop!' Fred would stop and pass me the bottle and so on. If they let you have a big drink, you might let them have a big drink on their go, but sometimes when the bottle reached their lips you would shout 'Stop!' straight away and they only got a sip.

We never had any of these bottled fruit juices or juice in cartons like today, so my dad made lemon barley for us. He would mix water, sliced lemons, sugar and barley in Mum's largest saucepan, all brought to the boil with the lid on, then left it to simmer for hours. When it had been cooled and strained it was put into milk bottles. Then we were allowed to help ourselves from the big jug on the dresser. The jug was an enamel one and when it was filled with our lemon barley drink it was very heavy so the boys would help me. Mum also made delicious sugar cakes. These were only pastry with a little sugar mixed in, then after they were baked a little sugar was sprinkled on the top. Mum would make these into different shapes and these were also on the dresser to help ourselves but we were not allowed to be greedy.

I used to love Sundays. Mum needed her kitchen to herself to make the Sunday roast dinner, so my brothers went to Cubs and Dad took me to see Auntie Ada and Uncle Jack. My grandmother lived with them and they always made us so welcome. Also I had Dad all to myself and to me that alone was perfect.

We all arrived home to that lovely smell of cooking in time for dinner and I could smell apple pie, my favourite. Dad would have bought a large joint of meat late on Saturday afternoon when there was a generous discount on any meat not already sold. The joint would be enough for three days as we would have what was left on Monday, sliced cold, on Tuesday in a shepherd's pie and on Wednesday, a beautiful stew with every vegetable you could think of.

So we all sat round our big kitchen table where my brothers played about, but they soon stopped when Mum gave them one of her looks.

Dad then very carefully sliced the joint and Mum put the vegetables on the plates. I was served first as I was the girl and the boys were being taught good manners. My mum was loving but really strict and both my parents insisted on good table manners. We would have to ask, 'Please may I start?' and 'Please may I leave the table?' It was so enjoyable all together round the table laughing, teasing and just talking. Dad always had a good story to tell, usually about when he was a boy. He used to go to the stream that in those days ran through Chiswick. Where the Windmill pub stands today was all fields then. He would go to catch tiddlers with his friends then go paddling with shoes and socks on. His mother never knew and when he got home he was in trouble because his shoes were ruined. The punishment was that he was not allowed to go fishing for two weeks and would get a smacked bottom. Poor old dad.

After dinner we went to Sunday school, and afterwards, when we walked home through the park, as we got close enough to our house to see our front-room windows, we would sometimes get really excited.

'Look!' shouted my elder brother, 'The big M card is in the window!'

'Oh yes!' yelled my other brother. 'So is the big W!'

The big M card meant muffins for tea. The muffin man used to walk round the streets calling out 'Muffins, muffins, lovely muffins,' and ringing a large bell. If he saw the M card in the window he would knock on the door and sell you some muffins.

The big W card was for the Wall's ice-cream man. He used to ride around on a tricycle with a big box full of frozen ice, and sell ice cream. When he saw the W, he knocked on your door.

The other good day was Friday, pocket-money day, when we all got one penny each. You could do so much with a penny in those days. I loved shopping in the In and Out shop where everything was under one penny, rather like the Poundland of today, and my brothers and I made a beeline for this shop. There were four farthings in a penny and so, for a farthing, I could buy a little celluloid doll with moveable arms and legs for my dolls' house that Dad had made me, a toffee bar, and lots of other things with the half penny left. They sold most things from toys to clothes and even household items. I got a pair of gloves there for one penny once. It was like a bazaar and what was so nice was they welcomed children in and made us feel important.

Woolworth's was a very large shop with a motto of 'nothing over sixpence'. It was a child's dream if you wanted to buy Mum or Dad a birthday present. My mum loved perfume and I could buy this in Woolworth's for six pennies. I remember buying her a perfume called Evening in Paris. It was in a small dark blue bottle about two inches high, shaped like a pear. I believe you can still buy it today but it is a lot more expensive.

The toy shops were fun with all the clockwork models on display, especially the train sets. They always included a dolls' hospital where you could get your dolls mended. When you collected the doll, she would always have a pretend bandage around whichever part had been broken.

As our parents were too poor to give us much pocket money, one way of getting extra was to go round all the red public phone boxes and press button B. In those days a telephone call cost two pennies. You put the money in the slot, dialled your number and when someone answered you'd press button A. If there was no answer, you'd press button B and get your money back. Of course a lot of people would forget to press button B and so there was always a chance we could get the money. It always felt exciting doing this – like winning on a slot machine.

We'd offer to do errands for neighbours and, because we had no telephones, one neighbour had a novel way of letting us know when she wanted an errand run for her. She would put a newspaper in the window and as soon as it was spotted one of us (usually Freddy) would ring her bell and take her list of errands. He would get a few pence in return.

There were two other ways we could easily make money. The boys used to go out with a bucket each and shovel up the horse dung on the streets. They sold it to people who had allotments and wanted fresh manure.

The second way was to knock on neighbours' doors and ask if they had any bottles to return. Soft drinks were sold in glass bottles and if you returned the bottle you got some money back. The neighbours were pleased to get rid of the bottles and usually said you could keep the money. Tizer was 4p with 1p back on the bottle, so it could all add up nicely.

We made our own fun out of whatever was around. My brothers made a board like a dart board but it had square hooks in it and you had to throw big rubber rings onto the hooks. There were numbers above the hooks and you added up the numbers and the highest would win.

My dad used to play with us sometimes and he made a shadow show. He would stand two books up on end, and put a thin book on top to make a small tunnel. He would get a clean hanky and shut one end of it in the top book. He would then take a torch, put the light out, and the show started. With the torch behind his hand he would make different shapes: a horse's head, an old man with a pipe, all sorts of funny things, and all we saw was the shadow on the hankie.

Dad was brilliant for making different things to amuse us. He would get one of Mum's plates, turn it upside down, light a match underneath so the plate turned black and with the match he then drew pictures on it. This was frowned on by Mum as it marked the plates.

There was one time I couldn't understand why I was not allowed in his shed. This was funny because he used to love having me in the shed and telling me how to make things. On this occasion, the boys could go in but not me. I was very upset until one day he said, 'Doris, you can come in now'. Do you know, he had made me the most beautiful dolls' house with real glass windows – I was so excited I wanted to cry!

My dad was so clever with his hands; he made the boys scooters, go-carts and the most wonderful fort with a drawbridge that really worked. It cost nothing but my dad's time, for the greengrocer was only too pleased to give us his orange boxes for maybe a penny, or usually for free, and this was the wood my dad turned into wonderful toys for us.

My youngest brother, Fred, was my pal, my playmate, someone I could go to when Mum was cross. There was no money for expensive toys and so most of the time we made up games and used whatever was lying around. Fred used to think up some lovely games. He would stand books up on end on our big kitchen table, then put Mum's tablecloth over them and we would have mountains. Then we would sit each end of the table and with our building bricks create our forts half under the tablecloth so we couldn't see each other.

Then we would play war and our toy soldiers would fight each other. This was a good game and kept us amused for hours. Fred was also the one who would play Snap or Snakes and Ladders with me.

My brothers used to go over to the park and chalk cricket stumps on a tree, then with a piece of flat wood play cricket. Us girls would have a skipping rope; one girl each end to turn the rope and the other girl running through the rope – if you couldn't get through and stopped the rope you then had to turn the rope and let the other girl in.

Sometimes we would be naughty and knock on someone's door then run like mad and hide in someone's front garden to watch the person open the door looking around in puzzlement.

We called the cinema 'the pictures'. We had a cinema near us, which showed children's films on a Saturday morning for a small entrance fee.

The boys were always playing about in the pictures; if a girl was sitting in front of them they would put all their toffee papers in the hood of her coat. Woe betide the girl in front of them if she had plaits as they would tie them together.

My brothers worked out if one paid to go in, they could let the other in through the fire door. They did this for a while until Mum found out. They were punished by not being allowed to go to the pictures the next week. This was disastrous for them and they promised not to do it again.

The cinema was so different then. For one thing all the films were in black and white only. There were three types of film: 'U', 'A' and 'X'. The U rating allowed anyone to see the film. The A rating was for adults, or young people accompanied by an adult. So you would get these children asking complete strangers if they could come in with them and showing them they had money for themselves in the palm of their hands. X-rated films were for adults only and I seem to remember they were mostly horror films in the 1930s.

At the beginning of the programme, the organ would be playing for a while and then as the first film was about to start, the organ slowly descended into the floor and the music became fainter as the Pathé Gazette News came onto the screen. Following the news you would then have a 'B' film which was a small short film with unknown artists, as any well-known stars would never appear in a 'B' film. Next would be a trailer for what would be coming soon. Then it would be the intermission. You knew when the intermission was coming as the organ started to play again, rising up from the floor.

All through the intermission usherettes would sell ice-creams, soft drinks and cigarettes. People would have a stretch, buy ice-creams or a Kia-Ora soft drink. A few ladies would also clean up, picking up rubbish and sweeping up any dog ends that had missed the ashtrays on the back of the seats.

You would get a couple of showbiz acts next for about ten minutes, and then at last the main film that you had really come to see.

The usherettes used to shine their torches along the back rows just in case there was any hanky-panky going on.

The programme was played on a continuous loop so you could come in at any time and stay until the film was back where you started.

As the war came along, this all changed and you only got the two films with the news in the middle. There were no toffee papers to clean up when sweets were rationed. You could buy a penny worth of broken biscuits so this was all a lot of people had to chew on in the tense part of a murder film.

If Mum and Dad took us to the pictures we would have hot chestnuts on the way home. The chestnut man had a steel or iron drum that had holes punched in it and a fire burning. There would be a tray on top with the chestnuts cooking. They had to have a slice cut in them or they would burst. Round the bottom of his drum would be the cooked ones keeping warm and ready to sell. A penny worth in a bag kept us three children quiet all the way home.

If we were lucky we would see the barrel organ man in the street with his monkey. While the music was playing the monkey would do tricks and collect pennies from us and sometimes even jump on your arm.

We didn't have many holidays when I was a child, but they normally involved an English beach and some very happy times in the summer, like a day at Southend or Brighton as they were nearest to London. The schools used to take the very poor children on coach trips but mum would never let us go. I believe once or twice Mum took us children to Bognor Regis for a week, then Dad came down on the Saturday to bring us home. Happy, happy days.

The little children used to have swim suits their mum would have knitted and they looked so sweet until they went into the water. Then the water got into the swimsuit and stretched the wool and made the bottom part drop so it ended up round their little legs.

Like a lot of middle-aged men, my dad would sit on the beach fully dressed with a hankie on his head. He would tie a knot in each corner of the hankie to make a hat for protection from the sun. If they were daring, some men took off their stiff collar and tie, but not my dad, although he did sometimes remove his shoes and socks. Mum would take her coat off but that was all – certainly no flimsy beach wear. If the sun got too hot she would wrap a scarf around her upper arms for protection. We all ran around on the beach and in the sea with no protection from the sun at all. We did get sunburnt and then calamine lotion would be smothered all over the burnt, red patches of skin.

I recently went on holiday to Bournemouth with my brother, and looking out of my window from my hotel I could see the pier. This brings back vivid memories of the Pierrots. These were a group of entertainers, dressed in white satin siren suits with a black ruffle around their neck and frills around the bottom of their trousers by their ankles, with black frilly buttons from neck to waist and a cone-shaped tall hat in white, with more frilly buttons from top to bottom in black.

There used to be a small stage near the top of the pier and people would sit watching in their deck chairs, with others standing around. The Pierrots were really professional performers: they would do comic sketches, dancing, singing, acrobatics, and generally entertain you. They might do three or four shows in a day. After their performance they would come round with a tin to collect money from you, as there was no charge for the show. You found a troupe of these performers at most seaside resorts. The people loved them and they always had a very big audience. I used to get mum to sit near them so I could watch them as I knew this is what I wanted to do – dance and entertain to be applauded. I will go on the stage, I promised myself.

***

Primary school was across the park from our house. It is still there today – Wendell Park School, a good school excellent for education. I was very happy there.

My dad used to take me in the mornings. He had a very big, two-wheeled truck with his name painted on the side. The truck was about six feet long, with hooks on the front either side of the handle for the buckets. There was a long handle for all his ladders, planks and tools. On the front were two big buckets in case he needed water for mixing the paste to hang wallpaper. Dad pulled and pushed this cart manually, walking to the next job on his list. I was so proud of my dad. He was very good looking, with a moustache that curled up at the ends. He stood there in his white apron that had a big pocket in the front. If I was lucky, there might have been some sweets in there too.

Every morning he lifted me up onto his truck, and as he was passing my school dropped me off there. This was such fun. I used to imagine I was a princess in my carriage. School came too soon; a kiss goodbye and he was off.

When Dad was unable to give me a ride to school on his truck my brothers used to take me, as we all went to the same school. Wendell Park School is a very large building. It was a mixed school but had separate playgrounds for boys and girls then. The playgrounds were next to each other but with a four foot wall in between. Another wall ran around the whole school about eight foot high so you could not see over the top. If you were playing ball and it went over the wall it was never thrown back so you had to be careful where you played. At playtimes my brothers would look over the wall to see if I was alright. They did this by one bending over and the other one standing on his back.

At the end of playtime, the old school hand bell was rung and you were called into school.

In the winter it was so comforting to come into a nice warm classroom. The desks were made for two pupils to sit side by side, and the seat was a fixture like a small bench. The desk itself had two sections, one for each of you, and an inkwell either side with one long flap lid to keep our work in, so you had to make sure when you opened the lid to let your partner know. The teacher had her desk facing you to the left, with a blackboard on an easel on the right. In the centre was a lovely fire burning all day, with a high guard all around it. Inside the guard were little bottles of milk warming up for us children. If you were the milk monitor you would put a straw in each bottle and the teacher would hand them out. They were never hot, just lukewarm.

Our classrooms were mixed but the boys were on one side and girls on the other with small gangways and a bigger one in the middle so the teacher could walk up and down. On arrival at school you had to line up in twos outside your classroom until the teacher came and opened the door with the usual cry, 'Quiet!'

When the register had been called, the bell went for assembly in the hall for prayers and hymns. This was also when the punishment book was read out. It was so shameful to have your name in the punishment book in case your parents found out and you'd be in real trouble at home too.

After assembly we had our lessons. These were very formal, one subject at a time, with no talking in class and certainly no playing, like the little ones do today. I was four and a half when I went to school and learnt to sit quietly.

Our schools were very tough. You could be writing at your desk and the teacher would come along and maybe see something she didn't like about your work, and then whack you on your knuckles with a ruler.

If the boys were talking in a lesson or playing about they could get the cane. If they did something really bad, like pushing someone down the stairs in a rush to get out for playtime, they could get the cane *and* their name in the punishment book.

If you were naughty in a lesson you would be called out to stand in a corner or made to put your hands on your head until teacher said you could take them down. Worst of all if you were really bad you would be sent to the head to be caned. The teachers had complete control over their class and us children only had to get one look from them to behave.

As the toilets were out in the playground the boys would pretend they wanted to go, giving the excuse of a tummy ache, and as it took a long walk it meant they could miss part of the lesson. After two visits though, the teacher would catch on.

Another thing the boys did in the toilets and everywhere else was to let off stink bombs. You could buy four stink bombs for just a half penny. They were little bits of blue paper with something smelly inside and when you dropped them the smell was disgusting; the boys took great delight in these.

We never had calculators but learnt our tables like a piece of poetry. Even today if I forget 9 x 9, I just run through the table and then know it's 81. Can children today do a sum without a calculator?

Most boys used to have a catapult and would roll up a piece of blotting paper, dip it in the inkwell and shoot it at someone. But we never had anything vicious like knives, only a penknife that had to be handed in and returned after school.

I remember sitting at my desk, head slightly bent down, my arm round my work so Ruby who sat next to me could not see what I was writing. The teacher came round and we had been doing sums. 'Sit up, Doris!' she said. 'Show me your work.' I had 8 out of 10 right but she just went, 'Mmm, yes'. Then she looked at Ruby's work. She had 3 out of 10 but the teacher praised her and I felt awful because I hadn't been praised, yet I had done better than Ruby. It seemed so unfair. Now I am older I understand she expected more from me as I was more advanced.

I became great friends with Ruby and as we got older we used to call for each other and walk to school together.

2

Secondary School Days
1938–1941

'Please, Doris, do hurry up!' That was my dad calling me to give me a lift to school in his big 'push and pull cart'. A quick glance down and, yes, my shoes were OK; they were dry. I had cleaned them last night with Blanco but being white canvas they took a long time to dry. It was my private dancing lesson that night. 'I'm coming, Dad,' I shouted. My dancing meant everything to me, especially now we were doing lots of shows and exams. At school playtimes I used to teach my friends easy dance steps and they loved it – we would bow, curtsey and put on shows for each other, even applauding; it was great fun.

I was ten years old and I never guessed what this day was going to bring for me. When my name was called out in prayers at school, my heart thumped. Your name was usually called out when you were in serious trouble. Then a boy named David was also called out and we had to go in front of the whole school.

The headmaster announced we had both won a senior county scholarship place. Gosh! I couldn't wait to run and tell my mother after school.

Running, running, wish I could go faster … must get to Mum … wonderful news. Nearly there, OK. Oh dear, a main road; I'm not supposed to cross a main road. But Mum wouldn't be angry, not with my news, would she?

Mum was working as a cleaner in a lady's house. I rang the bell at the side door (I wouldn't dream of ringing the front-door bell), and the lady who owned the house let me in and called Mum. Oh dear, Mum wasn't cross, she was livid! When I told her my news, she smacked me and said I was telling lies, then marched me straight back to school. The headmaster told her it was true and she should be proud of me. Of course, on the way home it was kisses, cuddles and sweets. By the time we got home the whole neighbourhood must have known.

The next step was taking me to one of the best secondary schools in the country, the Godolphin and Latymer in Hammersmith, as I still had to sit the entrance exam. The school was huge and the headmistress called a teacher to take care of me. Mum went away and had to come back in two hours. The teacher took me to a small room at the top of a winding staircase; she gave me a maths paper and a general knowledge paper. I also had to write an essay. She sat down in front of me and rang a bell saying I could start. I was so nervous but I finished all the work she set me. Then she gathered my papers and took me back to the headmistress. I was so pleased to see my mum there. The headmistress smiled. 'Thank you,' she said. 'We will be in touch by letter.'

The letter was a long time coming; at least two weeks. Then there it was on the mat; a big brown envelope. Mum had gone to work and I knew it was wrong for me to open it. So I had to leave it lying there and go off to school. It seemed as if 4 o'clock would never come. The bell rang. I started to rush out, but then I heard the headteacher say sternly, 'Doris, you will *not* run in the hall'.

Normally I didn't like my mum meeting me at school, as I was nearly eleven, but today was different. There she was waving something in the air; yes, the big brown envelope!

My results were very good. I was accepted into Godolphin and Latymer School. But, and there is always a but, I now had to go to County Hall for a medical just near Westminster Bridge.

The medical was very uncomfortable and they found I had a rupture in my groin, which meant an operation. Mum thought it was caused through ballet exercises but I would hear none of that, as no one dared to criticise my dancing classes.

So off to Paddington Green hospital for my operation. I wasn't so keen but it had to be done. On arrival at the hospital we were called into the office of the matron, who had a chat with mum, and my brothers had to sit outside in the corridor.

Then a nurse was summoned to take me to the ward. Mum could help me to settle in, but once again the boys had to sit outside. Mum gave me a kiss and a hug then had to go. Fred put his head round the door and put his thumb up. This made me want to cry but as my eyes filled up I said to myself, 'No, you are nearly eleven years old now. Be brave.'

But it was hard to be brave as I was very scared. The doctor came to see me with the ward sister and she reported directly to the matron, if there was anything of importance. Sister was in charge and all the nurses were a little in awe of her, I think. The doctor held my hand and told me all about what would happen and then he examined me and drew a line in my groin. I began to feel a little better as he was so kind. Then a nurse came and painted my tummy

29

with iodine, a yellow-brown colour, and covered it with a piece of lint. After an injection I really do not remember anymore.

The ward had about six beds, with a table at one end which had a reading lamp on it. This was for the night nurse who, when she came on duty, would turn out the lights and put on the reading lamp. The ward then looked really eerie, so dark and silent with the nurse sitting there at her table.

I was allowed home in three days but could not dance for ten days. On looking back I think that was the worst part of the whole procedure.

The trip to the school outfitters, Kinch & Lack, was much more enjoyable. I thought to myself, poor Dad, how will he pay for all this? It was alright though, because as I had a grant as well as the scholarship, he only had to pay one third of the cost. That was a relief! I still do not know how he managed it, as even a third of the cost was a lot of money to us.

I loved new clothes and the uniform was a navy gymslip with a flared skirt and a cream blouse. I could not believe the clothes list: indoor shoes, outdoor shoes, three pairs of gym knickers, gym shoes, three blouses, three summer school dresses, a hat, hat band, money purse. I also had a dark navy blazer with a school badge to sew onto the pocket, then finally from a different shop a tennis racket, a hockey stick and hockey pads.

I was all set for the big day in September. I felt so proud arriving at the school in my uniform. It was a beautiful old building and compared with my primary school absolutely huge. There were about twelve girls starting but only four were scholarship girls; the others were all fee paying and obviously had rich parents. We were taken to our classroom by a prefect and as the prefect opened the door, the teacher stopped talking and introduced us to the other girls.

I felt funny in my new clothes but it was a good sort of funny. My education had started.

At first, I felt a little uncomfortable, as there was such an obvious difference in the homes we came from. The girls arrived in their big cars, with leather satchels and nice lunch boxes; I used to creep down to the bottom of the playing field at lunchtime with my wrapped up sandwiches and brown paper carrier bag, with string handles. The carrier bag also had to hold my books, but books are heavy and they used to tear the bag. One Christmas, I was so delighted because I got a lovely brown leather satchel! Going back to school I felt as good as anybody.

I soon made friends with the three other scholarship girls. We went around together as a foursome and just ignored the looks we got from the 'paying pupils', who didn't seem to like scholarship girls invading their territory.

I was in the top stream for most subjects and I found the work so interesting that, in the end, my first year was really enjoyable. As money was tight, I used to walk the mile to school every day, but I didn't mind. Sometimes a bus would pass and I'd see girls in our uniform on their way to school and they would wave at me. If one of my three friends was on the bus they would get off and walk with me, so then we'd discuss our homework. We had a different teacher for each subject and I kept up with the work fairly well. We had a lot of homework but I made sure it was finished on Friday night, as no way would I miss my Saturday dance class. I had an agreement with Miss Merlwyn, that if I stayed to help teach the little ones, I would have a free half-hour private dance lesson myself.

In addition to my dancing lessons to look forward to, we had our shows at Chiswick Town Hall. Some of our show dresses and ballet dresses were so pretty and Mum would take me to the photographer in Hammersmith called Jerome's; three postcard sizes for one shilling. If you wanted colour it was daubed on gently with cotton wool. This was a real art and they called it touching up.

My life was happy, and as I made friends and became used to the new routine and different ways of doing things, I started to love school. My dancing of course was also a delight to me; I couldn't imagine life without it.

Then came the war and turned my lovely life upside down. It would never be the same again. My brothers and I were very, very scared. Mum was a bag of nerves as we had heard stories about all the children being evacuated; some stories were true and some not, but it really was a horrendous time.

We started to have siren practice at school in case the air-raid sirens went off. There were strict instructions: walk into the corridor, sit down outside your classroom in a line with your back against the wall and place an open book over your head. We were told the books were to protect us in case a bomb fell nearby, as the vibration could cause things to fall over or off the walls. I'm not sure how much protection they would have really given us. Of course when gas masks were issued, you had to put your gas masks on too. They were horrible and made you so hot. The sound of the air-raid sirens was loud and the noise used to be so shrill – it went round and round in a circle, up and down; you could hear it for miles around. The 'all clear' was better; just as loud but not so shrill and on the same note all the time. When we heard it there was such a feeling of relief. You could hear the planes coming, and then the loudest noise ever, if they dropped a bomb even a few miles away. So the 'all clear' siren was good to hear.

As the school was in Hammersmith, we had to be evacuated, first to Taplow in Buckinghamshire on a temporary basis for a few weeks, and then to Newbury in Berkshire. We left London from Ravenscourt Park tube station, with our gas masks in cardboard boxes hanging from our shoulders, a label pinned to our blazers and a carrier bag with a few biscuits, sweets and a tin of soup. Our mothers were hanging over the railings waving goodbye and everyone, yes even the teachers, were all crying.

It was really upsetting to be taken away from your family at twelve years old, not knowing where you were going or the type of people you would be billeted with. I was also so anxious that Mum and Dad would get bombed and didn't know where my brothers would be, or if I would I ever see my cat Woozy again. I hoped Mum remembered to feed him. It was a frightening time.

Somehow, after we were evacuated, school was never the same. You were just told where you were staying, with no choice, so you got split up from your friends and this made you feel so lonely. I cried myself to sleep many a time.

The school was based in Taplow for about six weeks. I was lucky as I was billeted with some lovely people who had a vegetable farm. My eldest brother, John, made a sign for their gate called 'The Little House'. He was so proud to see it when he visited me with Mum, Dad and Fred. My family had come down for the day on the Green Line coach and I was so excited to see them again! I was very happy in Taplow, but once our school moved to Newbury, I was moved again to a different home.

When we finally arrived in Newbury we were all ushered into a large hall, which might have been a church hall; I really can't remember. It was so scary – there were lots of children with labels on, like us; different schools grouped in corners with their teachers. As our names were called out, the hall gradually cleared. I was taken with another girl to a very nice house in a select area away from the town. We were introduced to our new

33

foster parents and the teacher left. We were told to call our foster parents Aunty and Uncle. Their names were Mr and Mrs Kilburn. Mr Kilburn was the manager of Woolworth's and they were extremely nice people. In fact, Mum would have called them really posh!

It was here I started finding out about good food. I had lime marmalade for the first time and it was delicious; I was addicted to it and still eat it today. Not that Mum didn't feed us well, she did, but this food was different. Mr Kilburn helped us with our homework and played cards with us. They had a son about three years old so life wasn't as bad as I thought it would be.

Although home life at Newbury was pleasant, I did not enjoy school so much at Newbury High School for Girls. We shared their facilities where we had the afternoons, and they had the mornings. We were split up into different billets, different classrooms, and walked different ways home so lost out on the closeness we had in London. So I never had a special friend to mull over homework with, chat about school and go around with. My shyness started coming back and I felt utterly miserable.

The paid-for pupils never spoke to me unless they had to; otherwise they just ignored me. They were probably decent girls but I just was not in their circle. There was one girl who used to say hello, but would walk away when her friends appeared. I was hopeless at sports and gym where the paying pupils were very good. I guessed they had lessons at home for tennis at their parents' club.

Yes, I just did not fit in. I wanted to get back into my dancing world where people were friendly and helped you. It was a pity as my work was up to standard but I think I was born to dance and that is what I wanted to do. Godolphin and Latymer School was a wonderful school and I was very lucky to have two and a half years there. Maybe, who knows, had we not had a war I might have stayed on at school, but I doubt it as my heart and soul was in my dancing.

However, after about six weeks we had to move again. I have no idea why but both Mr and Mrs Kilburn had tears in their eyes and hugged us so I think it couldn't have been anything we had done. After leaving them we were moved from pillar to post until finally we were split up and I was billeted with Mr and Mrs Thwaits. Oh dear! Another aunt and uncle.

Actually, Mr and Mrs Thwaits were very pleasant, but somehow I never wanted to call them Aunty or Uncle but always Mr and Mrs Thwaits. Mr Thwaits was a bank manager and although they were kind people with a little dog, I felt very lonely. Their house was very prim and proper, with everything in its place and quietly ordered. They had a nice clean house and I had a lovely little bedroom, small but comfy. I used to try and help by dusting their dining room, laying the table and washing up. Sometimes I would take their little dog for a walk. I believe he was a wirehair terrier, dear little dog.

One day on our walk a bull terrier seemed to come from nowhere; he must have jumped a garden fence. He got our little dog by the throat and although I am frightened of large dogs, I did try to separate them, but the bull terrier had locked his jaws not only on our dog's throat but also my thumb. A kind gentleman must have seen what was happening from a window and came running to our rescue. The owner of the big dog was upset and took his dog, then had a chat with Mr Thwaits later. How they parted the dogs, I'll never know. The kind gentleman told me to keep my hand up and carried our little dog home.

Mr and Mrs Thwaits were so kind to me and made sure I was alright. Mrs Thwaits dressed my thumb and Mr Thwaits went to the vet with the little dog. I was so relieved when he came back; luckily the dog had only caught the little fellow's skin and his throat had been stitched and we were told he should be fine. It was something I shall never forget as I was terrified, but Mr and Mrs Thwaits could not have been nicer.

I stayed with them for a while but this is when I started to get really lonely, and things began to go haywire. I missed my brothers so much, as being the youngest they had looked after me, played with me and stood up for me if anyone was not nice. I was surrounded by love at home but here I felt so lonely and miserable, even though my school work was going well. I slowly started to lose interest in school even though my maths was excellent. I think this was the time I was at my lowest ebb – I was so unhappy.

The headmistress had been very kind and let me practise my dancing routines in the hall for half an hour a day, for three days a week. I did appreciate this and it did help but a dancer needs music, a big mirror to see if she is doing the steps properly, new routines to learn, and either praise or criticism. Oh Miss Merlwyn I need you!

I was with the Thwaites for about nine months, and then I was told I was being moved again. I'm not sure why but I think it could have been because Mr Thwaits was retiring. So I decided I had had enough; I was now fourteen, which was the official age for leaving school, and I was going home, although Dad had signed to say I would stay until I was eighteen. Right or wrong, I needed to dance not stay in the classroom.

The problem was how could I do this? I had no money and I knew if I asked to leave I would be persuaded to stay. Then came my big plan. Tell no one; save my pocket money, and when I had enough, just go – run away. Mum would be cross, but I think this time she would understand especially as her wedding ring had been in and out of the pawn shop over the years to pay for my dancing lessons. From such a young age I had lived to dance and enjoyed every minute with my ballet or tap shoes on my feet, a little music, and then I was in another world of happiness. It really was all I dreamed about: to dance on a big stage, with a band in a big theatre. So my secret plan was put into action. It took a while to save for my ticket but finally the day came. I remember going to school in the morning and then just walking to the station and getting a train about 2:30pm. I had my books and a very small case with bits and pieces in. I arrived in London just as it was getting dark.

My plan was to phone a neighbour, Mrs Rogers, to go and tell Mum where I was so she could come to collect me. Suddenly, as we arrived at Paddington, I started to feel nervous, and felt like crying. I had to keep telling myself not to be silly. The train stopped, people were pushing and jostling onto the platform, and in the hubbub a lady's gas mask fell off her shoulders. I picked it up for her and she said 'Thank you dear' in such a kind way that, funnily enough, I felt better.

Now for that phone call. I was actually shaking but Mrs Rogers was a really lovely lady with her own children so I think she understood how I felt. She told me to wait while she fetched Mum from the house, so she could speak to me herself. Oh, I never ever thought how good it would be to hear Mum's voice. She told me to stay in the coffee room and speak to no one; she was on her way and she was *really* cross.

But when she arrived, oh what joy! She hugged me so tightly, it hurt. We both had tears running down our cheeks; we must have looked a funny couple, as Mum was born with one leg shorter than the other so had a limp, and we were holding onto each other so tightly that we kept bumping into everybody.

At last I was home. Mum phoned the headmistress in Newbury to tell her where I was and then the trouble started for poor Dad. He was fined five pounds for taking me out of school as he had signed a contract for me to stay there until I was eighteen years old. He paid a shilling a week; poor old Dad, but he never complained.

I now had to sweet talk them into letting me go on the stage. Much to my surprise they both agreed as they knew how I loved to dance. A new chapter in my life was about to start!

3

The Dancing Years
1941–1947

Out I went and bought a paper called *The Stage* where all the auditions were advertised, which still exists today. This was a really good paper for the theatricals and I studied it from front page to back. My heart sank as I scanned all adverts. Nothing there for me; oh dear! This was not going to be as easy as I thought. Never mind my private lesson was the next day and I vowed to have a chat with Miss Merlwyn, my dance teacher, and take her advice.

Arriving for my dance lesson early, I went into the studio and did a warm-up session with another pupil. In came Miss Merlwyn. 'Oh! Doris, are you free next Tuesday? I would like to take you for an audition, if your parents wouldn't mind?'

'Yes, yes, I am sure Mum wouldn't mind,' I replied, hardly able to contain my excitement. Mum was so pleased for me and went over the road to the phone box to phone Miss Merlwyn and make arrangements.

I couldn't believe it: my very first audition and interview was with the famous Mr Sherman Fisher, who managed the Sherman Fisher Girls! They appeared all over the country at top venues, including the London Palladium.

Imagine, there I was, only just fifteen and arriving at Leicester Square to see Mr Sherman Fisher. I was taken into his office alone and he asked me a lot of questions like: 'Why do you want to go on the stage? Will your parents object to you touring? Are you prepared to tour the country?'

After this, I was shown into the rehearsal room and asked to put on my rehearsal clothes and tap shoes. I was so relieved to see Miss Merlwyn already in there. The room was very large with mirrors all along one wall and bars on the side walls for ballet exercises, a piano in the corner and long forms (backless benches) to sit on. I thought it was badly lit as there were bare bulbs hanging from the ceiling without shades but then Mr Fisher came in and switched on all the spotlights and they were so bright it was like being on stage. 'Come on, dear, roll the tap mat out, give the pianist your music and show me what you can do,' he said encouragingly. I started my dance routine but halfway through he said, 'OK, that will do. Get dressed and come back to my office.' And off he went.

He hadn't let me finish my routine so I was anxious that he hadn't liked me. Miss Merlwyn said, 'Don't worry, you danced extremely well', but I wasn't convinced and thought I had ruined my chances. Back in his office, Mr Fisher smiled at me and said, 'I have a show going out – can you start rehearsals on Monday? You'll get to meet the rest of the girls then.'

Oh yes, yes, I had made it – I was going on the stage! On leaving his office, I heard him talking on the phone and he said, 'Yes, Mr Grade, I have my eight girls'. And to think I was one of them!

The next three weeks were really hard work. I had to travel from Shepherd's Bush to Leicester Square on the tube, and be there by 10 o'clock every morning. What with air raids, hearing bombs falling in the distance, small fires here and there from the incendiary bombs, it was quite scary. My Uncle Jack had already lost a leg putting out an incendiary bomb but Londoners just kept on going and I was doing what I was born to do – dance. Our new routines were soon learnt with hard practice and then finally we were off to Edinburgh for my first show.

Everyone in the show travelled together. We had a 'train call' and when the train came in, four carriages had labels on the windows: 'Reserved for "The Sunny Side of the Street" Company.' Look out folks – here I come! I was a professional dancer at last.

The air raids were getting worse and more frequent. My friend Ruby, who lived a few houses away, and I joined a small youth club the other side of the park. I knew I wouldn't be able to go very often as I was touring in a couple of weeks, but I joined anyway as quite a few of my friends went. It was good fun; they had ballroom dancing and upstairs snooker or darts. I was sitting chatting when this extremely good-looking boy came over and asked me to dance. His name was Austin and I became so self-conscious it wasn't true. After the dance he went upstairs to play snooker. I kept glancing up to the balcony out of the corner of my eye and, yes, he was peeping over. I had two more Saturdays when I was able to go to our club and couldn't wait – would he be there? Yes, he was, and we danced a few dances, then he walked Ruby and me home through the park. The last Saturday before I left on tour, addresses were exchanged and we promised to write to each other. When I was next home he took me to the pictures and we became good friends. He held my hand in the pictures – I would have liked to have stayed there for ever, but he hadn't even kissed me yet as he was quite shy. Whenever I was home he would come round and Mum really liked him, much to my surprise. We wrote letters and had dates but unfortunately, as I was away so much, it didn't last. He did say to Mum, why did you let her go on the stage?

But we girls did have some fun even when we weren't touring. When I was a teenager Friday night was always 'Amami night'. This was a lovely shampoo and wave set, and most girls washed their hair on Friday night ready for it to look nice for the week-end, especially if we were going to the Palais. So it became a saying, 'I can't come out tonight, it's Amami night'.

The Palais de Danse in Hammersmith was the heart of every-thing, *the* dance hall for a Saturday and Sunday evening – air raid or not – that is where you went for enjoyment. Most of the men were in uniform and when you danced with them you could feel the roughness of the fabric. The Americans, or Yanks as we called them, taught us to jive and as a dancer I loved it. I was lucky and had a good partner; we would go to a corner of the dance floor and jive away, until we were sent off the dance floor because jiving was not allowed. Sunday afternoon was for the serious ballroom dancers; this was called a tea-dance session. My eldest brother, Johnny, was a very good ballroom dancer so he used to take me there, looking so handsome in his naval uniform that all the girls were making eyes at him. We danced so well together and he used to practise new fancy steps with me.

It was Johnny who introduced me to his friend Jimmy, when they both came home on leave the same weekend as I was home from touring. Jimmy was also a sailor and he took a liking to me so we became pen pals but unfortunately he was killed in the war. Johnny said he was reported missing presumed killed. It must have been horrific for mums who lost sons and children losing dads, especially if it was the dreaded telegram or letter giving them the sad news.

I had a great friend named Freda from the company. As we stayed together all our dancing years and looked after each other, we became the greatest of friends, and our friendship lasted all our lives. She sadly lost her brother. He was on his way home on leave when his ship was attacked and went down. Freda was devastated, I tried to console her but in this hateful war all you could do was take it on the chin. I was always worried in case my brothers got hurt and listened to the news hoping their ships wouldn't be mentioned. When Johnny was discharged he called his house 'Calliope' after his ship.

How these sailors coped with months at sea I'll never know – I was seasick just sailing to the Isle of Man for our summer season! There I saw cats with no tails and thought they had been in a bombing, not realising that was the breed. The island is also known for its kippers and the fish shop would pack them nicely and send them to anywhere you wanted. I sent Dad some; he said that they were the best he had ever tasted. I was seasick on the way home too; I'd never make a sailor.

So when we were on leave, we knew how to enjoy ourselves dancing at the Palais. It was here where girls met boyfriends, where the war was forgotten for a little while, where future husbands met wives to be; where Yanks met English girls and married them and took them home to America.

My feelings for the Palais are of such happy memories; we danced all through the noise of guns and sirens and ambulance bells. It was the place where us young ones could forget the war and enjoy ourselves, meet our friends and have fun. We were called by the older folks the forgotten teenagers, as so many young men had been called up to the armed forces and young ladies were in factories making ammunitions.

We were working with Naughton and Gold from The Crazy Gang, who were top performers, as well as other well-known celebrities. We were told to be at the theatre on Monday morning at 9 o'clock prompt for a wardrobe call with a band call afterwards. We were to open to a full house on Monday night. I could hardly contain my excitement.

As soon as we arrived in Edinburgh, we had to find digs. I paired off with Freda, and we knew the stage-door keeper always had a list of suitable digs so we trotted off to the theatre.

The theatre amazed us! The name of the show was written in huge letters across the front. Normally this would have been in bright lights but not now because of the blackout. There were photos outside that had been taken previously and there we were, Freda and me, next to each other in the troupe, dressed in white military dresses with capes and hats. We both grinned, and loved it.

Digs were found after trailing around the streets. It was £1.25 for the room and we were to do our own shopping for food but our landlady would cook it for us. She was a little jolly lady with red cheeks and mothered Freda and me all the time we were with her. We put ten shillings each in the kitty for our shopping, which was plenty for the week.

We had an early night, first of all checking we had our make-up organised, or rather I should say greasepaint. It was like coloured candles, but it was special make-up and sold by numbers. I used 5 and 9 mixed together to make a lovely foundation and then there was eye shadow and lipstick. It had taken me a long time to get the right colours as I had fair skin. Dad had made me a beautiful make-up box with sections to fit the different make-up articles and a mirror in the lid. The final thing he painted was my name on the lid. We thought 'Dorice' was classier than Doris and sounded more like a professional dancer. So Dorice I became.

We got through band call and wardrobe with little trouble then went out for lunch and a look round Edinburgh. I couldn't wait to get back to the theatre for the show that evening. German planes had flown over twice in the afternoon but they passed without bombing. German 'look-out planes' used to come over but our boys shot them down if possible, so you heard a lot of gunfire.

Walking in through that stage door, I had the most exhilarating feeling ever. 'Evening, girls, let's hope it's a quiet night,' said the stage-door keeper. He meant no air raids. 'Your dressing room is number 8.' Number 8 was a good climb up a few flights of stairs, but I didn't care, I was young, fit and in the theatre with my first real show in an hour's time.

'Five minutes girls,' the call boy shouted as he knocked on the door. We hurried down the stairs onto the stage and peeped through the curtain; the house was packed. Lots of soldiers, air force and sailors in; I guessed they were on leave. The ladies looked so lovely, the gentlemen were very smart and the little girls wore pretty dresses. Blow old Hitler; tonight is going to be one I will remember all my life. There goes the curtain call; here we go!

We took up our positions on the stage; the footlights were so bright there seemed to be lights everywhere. Swish went the curtains and our routine started; we made no mistakes and kept time with each other. It was my first appearance on the boards, and the audience were clapping and clapping and clapping! From the stage you could only see four or five rows into the audience; the rest was like a fog, and you just about saw the shape of the dress circle.

The first half of the show went so well that there were whistles and shouts of 'More! More!' Then that dreaded siren went off. The theatre manager came onto the stage to announce there was an air raid and if anyone wished to leave, please would they leave now – but the show would continue.

Only a few people left and the show started again, which gave our comedians something to joke about. We did the rest of the show through the air raid; you could hear the planes, the guns, but thankfully no bombs. I guessed they were on their way to London.

We were in the middle of the finale when the 'all clear' sounded. Everyone cheered as the curtains closed and you could see them dancing in the aisles to the exit.

For me, what an experience, as apart from the air raid it was a wonderful night. Freda and I walked on air, home to our digs and, boy, did we enjoy our sausages and chips!

The next morning, our landlady was so nice when she asked us sweetly, please could we wash our legs before going to bed as the 'wet white' stained the sheets. The 'wet white' was like a tan we put on our legs; you bought red ochre and yellow ochre from the chemist and mixed it to the shade you wanted with water and a little liquid paraffin. Then you slapped it all over your legs. Freda and I had been so exhausted we had flopped straight into bed after supper. We just about managed to say goodnight to each other, but forgot all about washing off the 'wet white'.

While I was in Edinburgh my dad got caught in a bomb blast, which half-buried him. So I travelled back to London overnight on the Saturday to see him. On the journey, when I changed over to the tube train, there was a man in the corner who kept staring at me. He was slumped down in his seat with a loose dark coat tied tightly with a belt. I felt so uncomfortable with him staring at me that I got out of the tube train and caught the next one.

Poor Dad was black and blue, and also deaf. Thank goodness, the doctor told Mum he would completely recover in about three weeks. So as Dad was not too bad and I had to join my show in Brighton on the Monday, I planned to meet up with my old friend Ruby. We went dancing at the Hammersmith Palais on the Sunday evening. We were having a great time chatting to each other and laughing when someone tapped my shoulder and said, 'May I have this dance?' On turning round it was the man from the tube but he didn't look so scary in the bright light with the music playing. That evening we had a few dances and he walked Ruby and me to our bus stop. Of course, I now knew his name was Reg, and that he knew I was a dancer and what show I was in. At the time Reg was a commercial traveller and after that first meeting he followed the show round. Every night I would peep through the curtain to see if he was there. After the show I would run out with the girls around me, so I could miss him. Sometimes it worked, but sometimes he spotted me.

Another exciting audition was for a musical called *No, No, Nanette*, but only eight dancers were required. We were all called into Mr Sherman Fisher's rehearsal room and stood in a semi-circle of sixteen girls, waiting for the producer to arrive and pick the girls he wanted. Mr Fisher walked around us taking in how we looked. When he got to me, something was pushed into my hand; it felt like a cigarette packet. I glanced down and yes it was just that, with the words 'Go to wardrobe' written on it. My heart sank. Gosh, am I out even before the producer gets here? Off I ran and our darling of a wardrobe mistress said 'Come here', and quickly popped cotton wool into my bra. What a relief; I hurried back just before the producer arrived.

One by one eight girls were asked to leave, very politely, but my stuffed brassiere and I were in! Oh, what a lovely feeling. The show ran for eight months. By now, Mr Fisher kept us eight together for most shows as we worked and looked great in a troupe.

Between shows and summer seasons, he would put us in variety. This was a show but with different acts. In one of our shows was a woman called Karena. She had three alligators and played with them on stage, with her head in their mouths and all sorts of things. These alligators were kept in a tank on the side of the stage. Just before she performed we were on stage with a military number. In the number the music stopped and we tap danced without music to a certain beat. Now the alligators hated this and used to lash about in their tank, so we were scared they would get out, but they never did. Our military number would get enormous applause. Maybe the alligators were applauding too, who knows.

When you go for an audition and are picked out to join a show you have to sign a contract. One of the main clauses is that you must not change the colour of your hair. I was a mousey brown and was longing to go blonde as this was the fashion. So when the run of the show ended, we had a four-week rest period before our audition for the next show.

Ha-ha – my chance to be blonde! So Freda and I went off to the chemist. There were no hair colour dyes on the market at that time, so you had to mix your own. When I look back it's a wonder I have any hair left! To go blonde, I used 10 volume peroxide and some ammonia with some sylvan flakes. Sylvan flakes were flakes of soap and at this time they were the in-thing for washing woollens because they were so mild. This was all mixed up into a paste. You only used a small amount of ammonia and if the paste was too thick you just added a drop or two of water. Then you applied it to your hair, and sat in front of a mirror, watching the colour change. As soon as it was the right colour you had to quickly wash it off. The longer you left it on the more blonde you went. Some girls went platinum but I thought it looked like being grey. I wanted to be a golden blonde, so this paste was washed off quite soon.

Lucky for me when we went to our rehearsal rooms for auditions, Mr Fisher liked it, so from then on I was blonde. I'm still a sort of blonde today but use proper hair colourant from the chemist. When I look back I shudder to think the paste I made and the smell of the ammonia. I will admit though it did the trick. The shampoo I used was Drene – it came in little bottles enough for two washes and was advertised as 'Drene, the shampoo of the stars'.

Freda and I were both quite slim and we both had small breasts. One day we saw a cream advertised to make them grow so we would look like Marilyn Monroe. This sounded so good! I said to Freda, 'Shall we send for some?' She agreed and next day we sent off our postal orders and waited eagerly. After about ten days our cream arrived; it looked fine, a greasy white cream in a small jar.

We used it just before bedtime; Freda first, then she threw the jar over to me to use. This we did for about three nights, then one night we forgot until after we had switched off the lights. I gave Freda a dig. 'Oh dear,' she said, 'can you reach it?' The room was dark and I did not want to get out of bed to put the light on, so I sat up, fiddled around in the bedside cabinet and found the jar. I passed it to Freda to use and she passed it back for me to smear it on. That done we both went to sleep. The next morning the bed was in such a mess: everything was black, our nightdresses, the pillows, the sheets and our hands. I had only got hold of the shoe polish! Freda was the brave one who went and told the landlady, and believe it or not she just couldn't stop laughing. We both looked like chimney sweeps and it was the polish on our hands that had caused the trouble. We decided we best just keep padding our bras.

The theatrical landladies were always good sports and jolly souls. If we found nice digs on tour we would pass on their addresses to the stage-door keeper, who would then recommend them to others.

However, it wasn't always easy finding our own digs. We arrived one week in a town when it was mid-afternoon and raining. Freda and I had not booked our digs but we had a few addresses we could try. We asked at the station where the streets were and they directed us. So off we went in the rain, but after trying several places we could not find any vacancies so decided to find the theatre and see if anyone was there and could help us. Luckily the stage-door keeper had just popped back to collect his pipe and paper which he had forgotten. He explained that the night before they had had a very bad air raid and the company had to stay over as the transport had been disrupted but would be moving on tomorrow when the theatrical digs became free and we could then book in. However, as there were two of our girls already inside, he said we could join them and sleep in the theatre. We were so relieved. He took us in; it was so dark with just a couple of lights at the back of the stage but before we could ask any questions, he said 'Cheerio, see you in the morning!' and off he went.

We were all a little scared, so started messing around on the stage, imitating the stars of our show. We soon got tired and started to look for somewhere to sleep. We found a huge front curtain and all four of us snuggled in together, but just as we all got as comfy as we could, the air-raid siren sounded and we heard the planes overhead and the gunfire. I felt Freda trembling and put my arm round her, then in the distance a loud noise – it was a bomb dropped not far away. The noise was like a big rumble so very frightening, but thank goodness about half an hour later the 'all clear' sounded. We all slept badly as the theatre was very dark, and the noises were very creepy. I guess it was the wind and the rain blowing but as I felt so nervous, it made me think actors from the past were trying to entertain us. I still wonder. We were so relieved when morning came.

The stage-door keeper arrived with tea and toast for us from the cafe around the corner and had even booked us into some theatrical digs. He was such a charming man and looked after us the whole time we were there. 'Did you sleep well?' he asked, with a twinkle in his eye.

Pantomime was always lovely to do as it was so good to interact with the audience. We only used to do two or three numbers but we were on the stage quite a lot. This was called 'dressing the stage'. During a village scene while someone was singing, you walked about pretending to talk. Christmas was such a super time; I loved the hustle and bustle with everyone so happy.

Performing in variety shows was very different as there were a lot of acts with our dances in between. Sometimes you didn't have time to go back to the dressing room and had to change on the side of the stage. The dressers (the ladies who helped us) would hold up our dressing wraps to hide us from the stagehands.

Musical comedy was my favourite, as it is a mixture of a story, singing and dancing, and sometimes if you were lucky you might get a small part. The music was super in *No, No, Nanette*, with tunes like 'Tea for Two' which sometimes you still hear. We had a full house every night and the applause at the finish was deafening. What a show – a real hit.

When the run of a show ended you got a couple of weeks off before rehearsals started for the next one. This was called 'resting', but really you were running around doing auditions to get into another show.

It was strange, my heart used to beat so hard when waiting to go on for a number, but once the music started it was like magic; put a smile on your face and away you go. There is nothing like it, such a wonderful feeling, without a care in the world but to just dance and hear the applause afterwards. Fantastic!

Sometimes we would get a note come round from the audience. 'Will the blonde second from the left have lunch with me tomorrow? I'll be at the stage door after the show.' Usually they would stand there with a bunch of flowers. If they were in uniform we never refused, because they could be off to fight at any time, but we always got one of the other girls to come along too.

If you were in the entertainment business you had to perform in ENSA (Entertainments National Service Association) to entertain the troops. If the army, navy or air force had a camp near the theatre they would come over and collect us in a forces truck and take us back. This was usually if they had a dance in their mess room that was going on until midnight. Our shows ended at 10.30pm so we did half an hour of entertaining, like dancing a couple of our routines, then afterwards we'd join in with everyone. The truck ride was hilarious, us in the back with a couple of guards, being bumped about all over the place through the country lanes to the camp. They treated us like stars and took us home after the dance finished to all our different digs so that we were safe.

We made a lot of pen pals but sometimes we might not get a reply and would wonder what had happened. That is when you had a little cry and realised what a horrid thing war is.

Poor old Reg had chased me all over England but I kept on dodging him. I really did not like him in that way, but if he was not there I missed him, then felt cross with myself. He was forever coming round to Mum's so got very friendly with my brothers, especially Fred, who was dating Barbara, a young lady who worked in the shop under Reg's mum's apartment. So when Reg got to know me properly he sort of came in the back way, you could say.

Reg would find out from Mum where I was, when I would I be returning home and what station I would arrive at. That's it, you guessed right, he made sure he was there to pick me up.

The one thing that drew me to Reg was that he was a gentleman who treated me with respect – a kiss goodnight made him happy. Never did he, as we used to say, 'get fresh with me'. He always opened the door for me, pulled out the chair at a table if you were going to eat and walked on the road side of the pavement. I cannot say how or when my feelings changed, but all I know is that I loved him because he was just Reg. He used to give me his sweet coupons, even though he loved chocolate himself.

Once when I was home from the latest tour, Austin came to see me but I already had plans with Reg, who at that time was just a keen friend. So Reg, me and my first love all went for a drink. I sat there with the drink on the table and one hand being held by Reg on one side and my other hand being held by my first beau on the other side. I was in a dilemma. I really liked Austin, but after a while I had realised that Reg was a patient man and I started to feel kindly towards him.

4

The War Years
1939–1945

'Wake up! Wake up! Doris! Doris! The sirens have gone.' Mum was shaking me awake and then rushed out of the room, shouting over her shoulder, 'See you in the shelter!' The war was playing havoc with our night's sleep. Mum had a small case packed by her bed with all the important papers in, and guess what was on top? Her packet of cigarettes. The air-raid shelter was in the park opposite our house; it had bunks for us to sleep in and it was funny how we each chose our own bunk and used the same bunk each night.

There were usually about twenty-five of us and we had our friendly air-raid shelter wardens, who counted how many came in and also counted you when you left. The wardens were usually ladies who were kind souls; they kept nervous people quiet during a raid, hugging them and holding their hand. In fact they kept us all happy with their cups of cocoa and homemade cakes, but sugar was rationed so if you wanted sugar you brought your own along. People were so friendly and bought jugs of cocoa, crisps and anything to share. We would sing all the modern songs to keep our spirits up, especially anything by Vera Lynn.

The toilets in the air-raid shelter were most peculiar. They were like a large double wardrobe with a partition in the centre making two small rooms just big enough for each section to hold one person. This was made of light wood, but no doors. Instead we had two heavy curtains, one each side. The actual loo was like a big metal bucket with a removable loo seat and lid, which was a bit wobbly. No flush but strangely no smell. I guess it was a chemical loo. Every so often I remember the air-raid warden checking to see if it needed to be emptied; if so the loo seat was removed and replaced with the lid, and the handle was the same as a bucket handle.

The toilet became a huge joke as when you spent a penny it could be heard by everyone and the people outside would sing loudly to save any embarrassment. There were a lot of cheeky wisecracks like, 'That's three times tonight Mrs Smith – you will have to lay off the gin!' or 'You shouldn't have had that last pint, Jack'. If you were out shopping and met a neighbour she might say, 'Please don't give your husband baked beans again tonight. Last night … phew, what a pong!' Just cheeky jokes with no malice, and everyone took it in good part. If someone wanted the toilet and it was being used and they had been waiting a long time, up came the song 'Why are we waiting?' Sometimes, rather than waiting, the gentlemen would borrow the air-raid warden's tin hat and go outside to use the children's toilets in the playground on the other side of the park.

We used to take a wet sponge in a toilet bag over with us, as there was nowhere to wash your hands so that was the next best thing. Oh, and of course your own toilet paper. With bombs dropping outside, planes overhead, guns going off, there was a sense of relief we even had a toilet, although every one teased you.

Everybody had to carry a gas mask wherever they went. This was a ghastly rubber mask that covered the whole face with a window to see through. It had bands to go over the head and was airtight. As you breathed in and out it made rude noises. We looked like elephants. The mask was carried in a cardboard box with a cord over the shoulder like a shoulder bag. Some people bought a box made of leather but this was quite expensive. The police would stop you if you had forgotten to take it with you. Even little babies had to have a gas mask, but theirs was like a big bag with an air pump.

After the war really took hold, a lot of people never went to bed, they just went straight to the shelter, even if there was not a raid, because this way they got a better rest without interruptions. The next morning people would amble home wondering if their house was still standing or if any of their friends had been killed. Then you would get home, put on the wireless and maybe Churchill would be talking and somehow hearing his voice would make you feel better; someone was fighting our corner.

During the war a lot of people didn't use the public air-raid shelters, but preferred to have their own in their garden. These were called Anderson shelters; a big hole was dug and reinforced with six corrugated iron sheets bolted together at the top, with steel plates at either end.

Inside people would store tinned food, drinks, bottled water, biscuits and all different things to eat. They would have chairs, stools and a table. Some people would have bunk beds. It would

56

be fitted out like a room as some air raids could last for hours. In fact, a lot of people would go down to their Anderson shelter to sleep anyway so as not to be disturbed if there was a raid.

On the sides of many streets they built big brick shelters: just four walls and a roof with a door. These were very useful because if the bomb dropped, even a good distance away, shrapnel would fly around and could get embedded in your arm or leg, even your face. This left nasty scars and was extremely painful. After the war people were proud of these scars and would see who had the biggest. A lot of people are walking around today with scars from where the shrapnel was removed. There was a lot of shrapnel in the streets in all sorts of weird shapes and sizes, and people would collect it and paint it as a souvenir.

Tube stations were very useful 'ready-made' air-raid shelters, and people would sleep on the platforms all night. If you were catching a train you had to be careful in case you trod on a hand or a foot.

When people were leaving in the morning with their blankets and pillows under their arm you could hear whispers like 'Hope the house is OK ...' or 'I wonder where my boy is'; all sorts of concerns, all sorts of people, good innocent souls trying to cope with this horrible war.

The doodlebug was like a small airship. When it was over our heads we would hear its special buzzing noise and then suddenly – silence. Everything went quiet and we held our breath, as we knew it was about to explode. You just waited for the terrible bang, hoping against hope it wasn't going to land on you.

I was coming home one night from the theatre and suddenly there it was, a doodlebug bomb over my head. How stupid was I? I should have stood still instead of trying to beat it by running to get home. I could see Mum at the door looking for me and there were tears running down our faces. It hit a house not far from us and we knew the family; a very sad night.

Once when I was touring we were working in Plymouth. The city was so badly bombed, with rubble everywhere in the streets, we wondered if the show would go on or if we would even have an audience. The theatre was slightly damaged, possibly through flying shrapnel, and of course the show went on and a good old British audience packed it out. We were doing an Eastern dance number and we wore flimsy, sequin bras and pants with net trousers. We were absolutely frozen as there was a hole in the ceiling and you could see the night sky above. As part of the dance, I had to hold my palm up, keep smiling and pretend I didn't notice the drips of water steadily leaking from the roof onto my hand. But we were all alive and kicking, and holes in the ceiling were forgotten in the delight of entertaining a wonderful audience. It was quite strange; if the sirens went in the middle of the performance, we would find most people stayed on to watch the show. It just seemed part of life, but as soon as the 'all clear' sounded, everybody shouted and clapped.

When I look back, the day you really knew you were at war and how it would affect us all was when the ration book appeared at the beginning of 1940. This was a small buff-coloured book about 4 inches wide and 5 inches in length; it contained leaflets inside explaining what you were allowed and when you went to the shop they would stamp off what you had used on your shopping. We used to hope they would forget to stamp off something by mistake, but this hardly ever happened.

Life was weird: sweet coupons, clothing coupons, coupons for everything. As I was touring I had to take my ration book to the town hall and they would give me emergency coupons for how long I was going to be away and tear the page out of the ration book with an official stamp on the back. When I first saw the amount of butter I could have for a week I could not believe it, I used to eat that in one day! The amounts were very meagre and we used to swap with each other. Things like, give me your sweet rations and I'll give you my butter ration; it was so funny, here we were at war and bargaining with coupons. It was not any good moaning, that was that; we just got on with everything and were thankful that at least we had food.

Then came the identity card; this was blue, slightly bigger than the ration book. Inside was all about you: name, age, address, any health scares, and nationality, as well of course a photo (which never looked like you anyway, or if it did it would not be a very good one).

So when going out, the essentials were identity card and gas mask, as at any time the police or Home Guard could stop you. The good old Home Guard was made up of young men, middle-aged men who had not been called up and older men and pensioners. The young men who were not in the forces were exempt for different reasons and a lot of them worked in factories making ammunition. They did a very good job and at night if you were out it was good to bump into them, as everywhere was so dark and scary; they would see you home right to your door.

Apart from the Home Guard we had groups of fire watchers, who walked the streets in our neighbourhood putting out small fires from the incendiary bombs. My dad did this and had his book for his rota on duty, plus a whistle. Then if he found a fire or any problem he blew his whistle and people would come running to help put the fire out.

As soon as it became dark, we had to put the blackout blinds on all the windows because you must never show a light or the air-raid warden would bang on your door. 'Put that light out!' they'd shout. There were no lights in the streets; it was pitch black so we all had torches. We used to get old car batteries and take out the small batteries from inside, warm them up on Black Bess (our oven with a small fire on the side) and put them in our torches.

Needless to say, although my dad was a builder and decorator, no one wanted any work done during the war, so money was really tight. We would do all sorts of things to save money from eating very small amounts of food to running errands for people, and of course if you saw a queue outside a shop you would join it regardless. A queue meant the shop would have something that was hard to get and even if you didn't want it you could sell it. I don't know what we would have done without dried egg, because the rationing of food meant we had very small amounts of all the staple foods. The one thing we missed most of all were sweets. I used to have my dad's coupons but even then it wasn't enough.

I wasn't home much during the war, as my dance troupe were touring England, appearing at all the Moss Empires scattered throughout the country in all the big towns. My brothers were both sailors and, when on leave, would come and see the show I was in. The girls used to touch my younger brother's collar for luck, or that's what they said but they really wanted to date him.

Touring in England was so exciting; a different town every week. On the train call every Sunday I would wonder what the theatre would be like; maybe there was another theatre in the town as well as the one where we were working. If that was the case it was good as it made us work really hard to draw the people in. Good reviews meant everything to us. I used to hope our digs were near the theatre and that the landlady would be nice. Will the town be large, will we have a Lyons tea shop? This was crucial as we met there with the rest of our girls for morning coffee and to chat about the show, our digs and anything that was important to us.

I remember pulling into stations and getting our cases off the rack above. Through the window we could see small crowds of people waving their autograph albums in the air, hoping to see the stars of the show. Freda and I would grab our cases then, with a little giggle, step off the train with the crowd whistling. Another little adventure was about to start. How I truly loved this life!

After settling into digs and meeting the landlady, it was a quick wash then off to find our way around the town. First we had to find where the theatre was for the important band call in the morning – we dare not be late for this rehearsal. Then it was off to find a Lyons and for some of their delicious tomato soup. Then it was back to the digs and to bed, still wondering what the week would bring.

Some of the towns were so badly bombed it brought a lump to your throat to see houses with no fronts and people's belongings scattered about, shops with their windows boarded up trying to protect their property and carry on trading. Freda and I used to get upset sometimes on train call as you would see the station full of our soldiers, sailors and airmen on their way back to base kissing their wives, sweethearts and mothers goodbye with the little children clutching onto their daddies, babies in their arms, their little faces rubbing on the rough uniforms. Oh, this was a horrible, horrible war.

On arriving at the theatre one day, I cannot remember which one, Freda and I saw a little girl sitting on the stairs that led to our dressing room. She could have been anything from eight to nine, maybe younger, and she moved over to let us pass. We said hello are you in the show; she replied no but my parents are. What is their act, we asked. They sing and play the piano, she answered.

The next day we went to the theatre in the morning to collect our mail and we could hear beautiful singing coming from the stage which sounded like a child, so, being curious, Freda and I went to investigate. It was the little girl having what seemed to be a singing lesson from her parents. It was so beautiful Freda and I sat in the wings and listened.

Now if I tell you who her parents were you will immediately know who the little girl was. They were Ted and Barbara Andrews; yes, you've got it, she was our own delightful star Julie Andrews. I often wonder if she remembers me and Freda from the Sherman Fisher Girls.

Halfway through the war the Americans came over to fight with us. We called them 'Yanks'. There was a song we used to sing, called 'Over There'. It was a really catchy tune and everywhere you went people were singing it; in pubs, factories, on the trains and buses. It was a good thing for the country and boosted our morale no end. The Yanks brought over nylons, sweetcorn, chocolate, peanut butter – so many different things. A lot of girls met their husbands through this and after the war went to live in America. This was before I met Reg and I wasn't allowed to date an American as I was young and my mum was very strict. So even though I was old enough to be on tour, I still obeyed my mum as I just knew she'd find out somehow if I went against her wishes.

That doesn't mean they didn't try and lots of men would leave a note at the stage door for me but I wouldn't go on my own, although a group of us might go out together just to have fun.

After a while my mum relented, as I was getting older, and said it was alright to date an American as they seemed to be nice boys. So Freda and I grinned at each other and said wow, good old mum.

Strangely enough that afternoon we went to a tea dance before the show and, sitting at a table by the side of the dance floor, we were approached by two Yanks. 'Hi, girls can we sit with you? I am Hank and he is Herman,' one of them said. 'Why not – I am Freda and this is Dorice,' my friend answered. We had a pleasant couple of hours with them chatting and dancing. They told us how they were missing America and their families. Too soon we had to leave for the theatre to get ready for the evening performance and, oh yes, they were coming to see the show. When the curtain went up, true as they said, right in the front row there they were laughing, waving, pointing and grinning at us over the footlights, enjoying themselves. The show went well and as we came out of the stage door we could see them standing there in the dark like two little lost souls when all I could think of was, *Oh, two lovely young men off to fight – I certainly hope they come back.* They became very friendly with us but we were only there for the week then on to the next town. It was quite sad to say goodbye.

Sometimes our boys and the Yanks would have a dispute – our girls flirted with them so our boys got jealous. The Yanks had gifts for us and their uniforms were so much nicer. The Yanks adored our pubs and were very generous, always buying the locals their beer. The children would march alongside them in the street singing 'The Yanks Are Coming' knowing they might be given some sweets.

There might be a war on but everybody was always ready to talk, listen, have a joke in those days – I suppose because you knew any of you could be bombed tomorrow. Today people can sometimes be so rude with a phone stuck in their ears – what's wrong with them? You never hear a 'good morning to you' these days.

The war seemed to go on for ever, but now I will tell you about when it was over. VE day on 8 May 1945 was unforgettable: lights on the street, fireworks, bonfires, people shouting and singing. I was at the Shepherd's Bush Empire and when it was announced everyone went mad: the audience came up on the stage and we all crossed hands and sang 'Auld Lang Syne'. People everywhere were kissing, cuddling and shaking hands. What a celebration, what a night!

Vera Lynn was called 'the forces' sweetheart'. She used to entertain the forces, singing love songs on the radio requested by their loved ones. She would travel abroad and entertain them live, even going into the war zones. One song she used to sing was 'When the lights go on again (all over the world)', and my how they did! The street lights came on, and all the shop windows once more were lit up. I think to most people pulling down the blackout curtains gave them the most pleasure, as it was a sign that war was really over.

Because I was appearing in a show at the Shepherd's Bush Empire, which was not far from where I lived, my dad came to meet me on the day war was declared over. Everyone was so excited out on the streets, and he was worried about me coming home alone after the show so late at night. Instead of taking the bus, we walked home and in all my life I have never seen people so happy. Strangers were shaking hands, kissing each other, singing at the top of their voices, waving flags and dancing.

That was a lovely memory, Dad and me walking hand in hand, laughing and joining in the fun. I was so pleased he had come to walk me home. As we reached the top of our turning

64

I saw Mum at the door looking for us. Then she spotted us in the distance and ran to meet us; being lame this was hard for her, but there we were, arms around each other in a circle going round and round laughing and crying. Oh my, what a night!

Freda and I loved to go shopping in the high street in Hammersmith after the war, now that the clothes shops had pretty dresses in their windows with so many styles and colours. There used to be several shops in the high street so we certainly had a wonderful choice and we could spend the whole afternoon walking up and down just looking; it was so nice to see the windows beautifully dressed and brightly lit after the darkness of the war years. We were treated like princesses and dresses would be brought to you in the changing cubicle – a really high-class customer service. When we tried on shoes they had a small X-ray machine to show you if the shoes pinched your toes.

The shoe shops were my obsession; I love shoes and wedges had come out. They were so fashionable which made a change, as during the war most people wore flat lace-ups, so if the siren went they could run faster to the air-raid shelters. Now it was a luxury to buy whatever you liked.

Just off the high street in a side turning you would find my Aladdin's cave, the draper's shop. This is where I would buy materials for my dance costumes. The shop sold ribbons of all colours, beautiful lace, feathers, sequins and of course buckram cloth, which was a coarse cotton fabric stiffened with glue for making our military dance hats. I also bought Tarleton cloth for wearing under a full skirt. I could fill a page with their stock, including dress-making patterns, knitting needles and knitting patterns.

Because I was in this shop most days the shopkeeper got to know me and of course my mum, who did a lot of knitting and bought all her wool from the draper's shop. If Mum was making something large like a baby's shawl or a cardigan, which would need a lot of wool and she could not afford to buy it all in one go, the kind lady would put all the wool required into a bag under the counter with Mum's name on it and sell her two ounces at a time. If she hadn't done this, the shop might run out of that colour and when the new stock arrived, the colour would be right but the shading might be slightly different and would show up in the article when completed. I miss the draper's shop because if I want just a small amount of ribbon or lace where do you go? The nearest to me now is a market, two bus rides away.

Shortly after the war the new look came in; this was a longer fuller skirt. All the girls went crazy as the clothing coupons were withdrawn and you could make your own dresses with cloth of your own choice. Goodbye, blackout material!

5

The Love of My Life
1941–1950

Isoon realised, as I got to know him more, that Reg was a true gentleman. He was always there for me and, when he was not around, I used to get quite lonely and start to miss him. So I stopped being nasty and we spent more time together. I found he was entertaining, even amusing, and we really got on very well. In time we met each other's families. Oh dear, little did I know the problems we would have.

Although John and Fred, my two older brothers, seemed to get on well with Reg, my parents did not approve as he was twelve years older than me and Jewish. Reg's mother made me very welcome but a Jewish home was very different from ours. One of the first things I noticed was that you are offered food all the time! Reg's step-father was choir-master at the Shepherd's Bush synagogue; a very charming man. I called him 'Papa Shoot' as his surname was Shoot. Unfortunately the two families just did not get along with each other.

After about two years, it was at the dear old Palais where Reg took me upstairs onto the balcony and asked me to marry him. I agreed, but how on earth was I going to tell Mum and Dad? Whatever they thought we were a couple now. I knew they would hit the roof; they did, and all havoc broke loose, so I ran out of the house and went to the pictures.

Strangely Reg's parents were OK about it. It was my mum who was difficult; she would not sign the consent form as I was under twenty-one, and at the time you could not marry without your parents' consent.

'I'll put my head in the gas oven if you marry Reg. He is too old for you and the religion is too different,' Mum shouted at me. I was crying – it was ghastly, I was just so upset. Then Freda, my best friend, said to Mum, 'OK, there you are!' and she opened the oven door, put a cushion there, and 2 pence in the meter, and pulled me out the house. We went to the pictures, but I couldn't settle as I was upset so we came home early and there was Mum, knitting, with the consent form signed. Freda and I looked at each other and Mum said, 'Well, put the kettle on, I want a cup of tea'. This was her way of letting me know that although our engagement could go ahead, she wasn't happy.

Reg's family were happy for him and accepted me. His sister Rene invited us to her home to celebrate, and as she was married to a Christian, they knew exactly how we felt.

On the way to Rene's, as we were early Reg parked the car and we went for a walk on Ealing Common. This is where Reg gave me my engagement ring. It was a solitaire diamond platinum ring and very beautiful. I told him I liked it and thanked him and said all the right things, but in my heart I didn't like it at all. It just didn't suit my small hand.

The ring seemed to make everything final; I was entering Reg's world which was so different from my own. Some people were quite hostile to us, even a few of my friends. This puzzled me and I could not understand why, as Reg's dad came over to England as a baby and Reg was born here. He lived in Bow and was as British as anyone else. We closed our eyes and ears to the prejudice and got on with our lives.

Slowly over time, Mum got used to Reg and was beginning to thaw. One reason I guess was because he gave her lifts and took her for car rides, especially to her loan club. This was where you paid money in every week then drew it out at Christmas. The loan club was usually in a pub so Mum got her gin and lime while Reg had a beer. This was a great asset, as with her shorter leg she was frightened of the blackout in case she fell. Reg kindly took her for a car ride every Friday and I did appreciate it, especially while I was away on tour.

As our relationship deepened, I realised how generous Reg was, not just to my mum, but to all his large family. We used to take his mum to Brighton, so she could visit her sister, Aunty Anne, who lived in a large house in Hove. During the summer she occasionally took in guests. While the sisters were chatting, Reg and I had a lovely day going round Brighton. He took me to the Lanes where his cousin Michael had an antique shop. I had never been to the Lanes before; all the shops sold antiques and the beautiful things amazed me. Cousin Michael was very distinguished and had a moustache similar to my dad's but smaller; he was very debonair. He gave Reg a glass of wine and I had a cup of tea. After a pleasant hour we went back to Aunty Anne who insisted we had a meal.

The day passed so quickly, and after our goodbyes we set off for home with Reg's mum in the back seat. Everything had gone so well; even the car started on the button so we didn't have to crank her with the starting handle. We were a few miles out of Brighton when a very heavy fog came down. Reg opened the car roof and tried to drive by putting his head out, but this was impossible so he had to turn round and head back to Aunty Anne. This took quite a while but we finally arrived back at her house, safe and sound.

Her house was full of paying guests, but she insisted we use the lounge and gave us blankets and pillows. There were two sofas so Reg's mum had one and I had the other. Reg had two big armchairs which he pulled over by my sofa. Quick as a flash, up popped his mum. 'Reg, pull those chairs back a bit,' she called. He laughed and did so, but just far enough so he could hold my hand all night.

There was no way I could contact my mum, as in those days there were no mobile phones. When we arrived home next day she was cross as she had been so worried but soon calmed down when she knew Reg's mum had been with us.

Another thing Reg and I liked to do was to go to Chiswick House to have tea and sit on the grass and just chat. Sometimes the children from the schools close by would have their sports days there which was nice to watch. Chiswick House has beautiful gardens, but one day Reg and I did not hear the closing bell as we were there in the evening and lost to the world chatting about our wedding. We suddenly realised it was getting dark and felt such idiots as we had to knock on the lodge keeper's door to let us out. That was not the worst of it; we had sat on an ant hill and had ants crawling all over us. Reg drove me home as quickly as he could and I went straight in the bath. What a good job my dad had turned the old walk-in larder into a bathroom! Reg did the same thing when he got home; I guess you can say we had 'ants in our pants', that's for sure.

When I got to know Reg a little more I found out that he liked a game of poker and he belonged to a card school. In our day if you played for money it was illegal but as they were friends or relatives I am afraid they went ahead anyway. Reg's sister Irene was always there as she too enjoyed a card game. Her husband John, who was Christian, didn't gamble but used to make sandwiches and tea. There was a pot for money on the side and the players put what they liked in for John, as he looked after the players.

Anyway, sometimes I would go along and watch; it was so funny to hear them moaning if they were losing and arguing with each other in a good-natured way. One night we went along for an evening's poker and rang the bell, but there was no answer. This was strange as someone should have been at home. The flat was above a restaurant which had a flat roof where they played. Reg was very concerned so we went into the restaurant to ask if anyone knew where they were. 'Yes,' they said, 'the police have arrested them.' Oh my goodness – poor Reg's face dropped a mile. Apparently while they were playing cards, the police came up onto the roof and saw them through the windows. Of course they had no excuse; money was in the centre of the table and cards were in their hands. Reg was so upset that we stayed in the restaurant until they all came home. Each person was very heavily fined, but guess what ... they were playing again the next night. Irene was forever talking about her ride in the 'Black Maria'.

One weekend when I was home resting, Reg and I took his mum to Shepherd's Bush Empire where Michael Miles was playing. He played the 'Yes and No' game where he asked the contestants questions very fast, but they weren't allowed to answer with a yes or a no. This was quite difficult as the questions were phrased so that you wanted to answer yes or no. He invited anyone from the audience to go up on the stage. Reg had always teased me saying, oh, anyone can go up on a stage. Now was my chance – I stood up and pointed to Reg, so he could not get out of it. There were six people going to have a go. Reg was fourth and did quite well but slipped up in the end. As a result he had to pay a forfeit and he was taken into the wings. After all the people had their turn, it was announced that a couple of professionals would be performing a quick step. The band played a very quick number and in came Reg with a life-size doll tied to his feet and hands. He jumped and hopped about all over the stage waving his arms and lifting his legs; it was hysterical. The audience were laughing and clapping; even his mum got excited. After that he used to tell people, oh yes, I've been on the stage too.

The day arrived for our two families to meet at last, to talk about the wedding. Reg picked us up in his car. My mum had on her best dress, which she called her two-guinea dress because that is what it cost and she had just bought it off her tally man. When you bought something at one of the large department stores you could agree to pay off a little each week, rather than pay it all in one go. The tally man called every Friday to collect the money. Mum looked so nice, and although she was very strict with me, she had a soft side and a very pretty face. I gave her a hug and felt quite proud of her, so off we went to meet the in-laws to be.

We were made very welcome; there was a table full of food in the corner and yes, as promised, Reg's mother had made me a cheesecake. Mum's eyes glistened; she loved creamy cakes. Much to our surprise it went off alright. I believe it was because Mum enjoyed the Jewish food and so much of it! She had never had smoked salmon, latkes or salt beef.

Yet, you could see the two mums didn't really like each other but were on their best behaviour. The wedding day was fixed for

22 April 1948, at Hammersmith Town Hall in the registry office. Although the war was over, things were still hard to get, but clothes were now 'off coupon' so I searched up and down the high street until I found a nice white coat with a navy trim and navy blue shoes, and I made myself a sort of headgear out of net, as I hated wearing hats. With a pretty blue dress in light wool, I felt quite satisfied. As a wedding present Reg's mum was giving us a reception dinner in a restaurant, which was ideal, so all I had to organise was buying a cake. This I had made by Fullers and it was superb.

The big day soon came round. I felt very nervous as Mum went ahead by taxi with some friends and Dad and I followed in another taxi. Then suddenly Dad did something I least expected. Half way to the town hall he stopped the taxi and asked me to call it off. Now my dad was such a quiet, easy-going man and never interfered in anything, so this was totally out of character. 'Dad, I can't do that!' I replied really shocked. 'All the people are coming.' 'That doesn't matter. I'll tell them, I'll explain,' he said quickly. I turned to him and said gently, 'But, Dad – I love him.' He tried for about fifteen minutes to stop me, but in the end he kissed me and said he was just making sure, as our age difference and our religion could make things difficult. Dear Dad, how I loved him. So off we went, arriving twenty minutes late as every bride should.

We arrived at Hammersmith Town Hall and the registry office was at the back, with steps up to the door. Mum was waiting there anxiously and rushed over to me. 'Are you alright, dear?' she asked. I nodded and we made our way up the steps; Dad with me, Freda with Mum, and then just behind came Reg's mum. She came over to me and squeezed my hand, and a neigh-bour's little girl gave me a silver horseshoe. Unfortunately, my

73

brothers could not come, as Fred was in America and John lived in Leeds, and he was not too well. However, there were about twenty guests, and it was heart-warming to see my dear old grandmother and great-aunt Lotty who were both in their eighties.

It felt peculiar in the registrar's room. Reg standing there looking so smart and formal but then he gave me a wink and I gave him a smile. We stood in the centre of the room with Freda on my side and Godfrey, Reg's brother, on his side, with the two mums and our dads sitting in the front row in a semi-circle, with the other guests behind them. The ceremony was very short but when I was asked 'Will you take Myer Greenfield to be your husband?', I thought who is Myer? We looked at each other and he grinned – he had forgotten to tell me his real name. Then to my amazement I saw that both mums were crying a little.

After the photo session on the steps outside, we all went to a restaurant for a meal in Hammersmith Broadway. This was the promised wedding gift to us, from my new mum-in-law. The meal was very good and we had a few speeches, and then off to mum-in-law's house to cut the cake and carry on celebrating.

At the house, you would never believe it! The Christian guests sat one side of the room, the Jewish guests on the other side. I must say I felt sorry for my mum-in-law as she was trying her hardest to give us a day to remember.

The cake was cut, the wine was poured and Reg and I passed it round. There was a nice speech and toast to the bride and groom, by one of Reg's family. Then someone shouted 'Mazal Tov!' which means 'Good luck!' in Yiddish. I guessed it must have been Papa Shoot.

We then said our goodbyes and left for Brighton in our old banger, which was now decorated in streamers and balloons. We had two nights at Reg's aunt's house. We could not afford a honeymoon but planned to have one later on.

All in all the day had gone off well. The two mums had behaved and everyone I think had enjoyed themselves.

***

So I became Mrs Dorice Greenfield. Mum had let us have her front room as it was impossible to find a flat, and we were sleeping on a put-you-up. Not so comfortable but at last Reg and I were together and getting used to married life. Reg was working as an electrician. He was trained for this as a lad and now returned to the trade he wanted. I was working at Osram's making baby valves for hearing aids, using a spot welder. Life was so different after being with theatricals and touring. I missed the company of my troupe and so wished I could dance again but, back then, once you were married you couldn't go on being a dancer as touring took you away from home too much. Freda was still with the troupe and we kept in touch.

The sort of food Reg liked was very different from the food I was used to, but there was a large Jewish delicatessen a short way away from the flat, which was a big help for me as I didn't have a clue what to get Reg to eat; the only thing we had in common was baked beans on toast. However, I soon worked out some sort of menu and Reg's mum was a big help. His sister was very kind and took me under her wing. Papa Shoot spoke in Hebrew and then his sister used to tell me what they were talking about so I didn't feel uncomfortable wondering what they were saying.

After we'd been married for a year or so, we settled into a happy routine with lots of new friends and we went out a lot. Unfortunately, our families were still hostile with each other in a sort of passive way. They never argued but they didn't speak to each other either, apart from hello or goodbye, unless it was something really important. They came from such different cultures and didn't understand each other.

During the first few years of married life, Reg and I had to adjust and respect each other's different culture. By now Reg was eating English food and I was eating Jewish food, so it worked out alright from the food point of view.

The first time I went into a synagogue was bewildering. It was to Reg's brother's wedding. The men wore little black skull caps and sat separated from the women. During the ceremony, the bride and groom were married under a canopy and then a glass was broken. Just the opposite to our Christian religion. In a room on the right, as you went in, was a long table and I have never seen so much food: pickled herring, smoked salmon, latkes, salt beef, every sort of salad and all of the finest quality; enough food to have fed more than the people there. Reg looked so smart in his top hat (he was the best man) and we all finished up at my mother-in-law's house and, guess what, yes more food. She even insisted Reg take some home and sent my mum a box of matzo biscuits, as she knew my mum loved these. They are big wafer-like biscuits and I was told that as the Jewish people were leaving their country they had on their backs the paste of flour for cooking and the sun baked it as they were walking.

Before we left the wedding reception, I helped Reg's sister with the washing up, and even this was a new experience. There were different bowls, as you were not allowed to wash anything milky with meat, so the meat dishes were washed up in one bowl and the sweet dishes in another, and there is one time in the year when one lot of china is packed away and a second lot brought out for use. After the bride and groom left, the party ended and we went home, but for me I had seen a little bit of Reg's culture. I loved it. I was beginning to get interested in the religion, which was so different from mine. Mum-in-law used to tell me interesting stories and we got on very well together, so much so that if Reg and I had an argument she always took my side.

Another new experience for me was keeping the Sabbath. Friday night in the Jewish religion was their Sabbath, which was called Shabbos. On this day they are not allowed to work, ride in a car or on a bus, nor even turn on the lights. They used to have prayers and a feast of lovely kosher food in the evening. Kosher meant the food had been specially prepared and blessed. They would leave the door open for a while in case a stranger might want to come in and would be welcomed to join the meal. Also a non-Jewish person could turn their lights on. We used to try and go to Shabbos, as it meant a lot to my mum-in-law for all her family to be there.

Jewish funerals are also different from the Christian religion. No flowers are allowed, and after the service the widow or widower would sit on a low stool at their home and wait to receive condolences. The rabbi would come and say a prayer and cut a part of their clothing with a small slit. When you came to see them to pay your condolences you had to say, 'I wish you long life'. For ten days after the funeral, ten men had to be present and prayers were said in the house where the bereaved person lived.

To me all this was hard to understand but through the years it became very interesting. My mother-in-law was so good to me and she would explain everything so I never felt left out of any of their rituals.

Reg told me about the years when he was growing up and things were not easy for a Jewish boy in a Christian school. He always thought his mum should have let him attend Christian

77

prayers but this was definitely not allowed, so he stood out from the other children. He was a nervous little boy, and used to be bullied which made him stutter. He was never asked to join in the other children's games.

There was real prejudice against Jewish people in those days. Reg was interested in electricity from a very early age, so after primary school he went to a school specialising in engineering. He was deeply unhappy, as people were so hostile that he didn't finish the course and one day he just walked out. He never told me he was Jewish when we first met, not until he really knew me. Even in the first years of our marriage, people could be very unkind. They would say to me, why did you marry a Jew boy? My answer was, 'I love him and to me all people are the same'.

Reg's life had been so different from mine and in the first few years of our marriage we both had to adjust. This was not so difficult for us, as if we had a different view on things, a kiss and cuddle would settle everything. It was the mums who were so distant from each other and didn't even try to adjust. My brothers and Reg's sister and brother were all very friendly. Freddy loved the Yiddish language and picked up a lot of words that he still comes out with today.

Godfrey, Reg's brother, was the richer of the two and if we were going to visit him and his wife Terry, we would dress up in our best clothes. There would be lots of Yiddish food and Reg would tuck in. Godfrey had a daughter Angela and a son Lawrence. Angela, although only five, would fill me a plate of food and bring it to me knowing I was not used to Jewish food, but picking out what she thought I would eat. I have always remembered this as it was so thoughtful and I was still a little uncomfortable meeting all the aunts and uncles.

Aunty Sophie was a darling; she used to tell me Jewish stories and when she first met me she said, 'So you found a nice Jewish boy then'. I liked her straight away; she was a fun lady.

Reg's sister Irene and her husband John liked to gamble and quite often would take us to the casino. We used to have to dress smartly and the men had to wear ties or they would not be allowed in. This amazed me, but Reg took to roulette like a duck takes to water, and so we joined too and became members. Once a month, you had a three-course dinner on the house, and this was super, as it all felt very grand to me. In the years to come we were members of most of the casinos along the south coast as Reg was always working out a new winning system.

If only our parents would call time and make friends it would have been perfect, but they never did. Mum-in-law was from the old school, very prim and proper with her own views on life, and funnily enough my mum had similar views (although she wasn't quite so prim and proper) – it was just that they did not like each other. Maybe there was a little bit of jealousy, as each one wanted to be the most important to Reg and me, especially when the children came along.

In the early years of my marriage I found out three things about Jewish culture: whenever you called at their house you had a really good meal, they liked a game of cards and guests were always made very welcome.

6

Settling Down
1950–2005

We stayed with my parents for two years after our marriage as flats were scarce, owing to the war and bombing, so it wasn't until January 1951 when we left '64' and moved with our young baby to 47 Chiswick High Road.

To be honest, it was a relief to move into our own home. It had not been too comfortable at Mum's: sleeping on a put-you-up in her front room and living so closely together created a certain amount of tension. Although by now Mum liked Reg, while we were all living together they did not get on too well. It was mainly my mum's fault but Reg didn't help the situation and I found myself in the middle as the peacemaker. Thankfully my dad was fine and there was no problem with him.

The problem was that Mum was used to everyone helping out with the chores; Reg had been brought up to expect the women to look after the house and do all the housework and cleaning up.

For example, he loved baked beans and used to eat them cold out of the tin, but instead of putting the tin in the bin, he would just leave it on the floor where he had been sitting. This annoyed my mum so she started saving the empty tins until one day she tied them all on his bike, round the handle bars across the saddle about eight times. You can imagine when Reg went to go to work what happened. He was so cross he had a big row with Mum. Another thing that annoyed my mum was that because Reg was always cold, he would sit really close to the fire and she thought he was being selfish. There were quite a lot of little incidents like this between them so it wasn't ideal.

When I realised I was pregnant with our first baby, we knew we would have to have more room, so it was a blessing when Papa Shoot found a flat for us in Chiswick. Papa Shoot had a small jewellery shop, and he heard from a customer that there was a vacant flat going on the first floor in Chiswick High Road. Reg's mum called Reg at work and he immediately went to see the flat; he then met me and we went round and accepted it. We had a home at last and we lived there for fifty-five years. The rent was £1 per week when we moved in but when we left it was £130.50 per week.

Our new flat was wonderful! It was in the middle of a large three-storey Victorian house. It wasn't self-contained; there were other tenants above us and the landlady lived on the ground floor. The upstairs people Ted and Alice (known as Al), 'the Macs', were rough diamonds, a little on the coarse side, and they had a large Alsatian dog. I was scared of Max the dog at first, as he used to sit on the top of the stairs looking down into our flat.

The flat had a kitchen in the back of the house and the kitchen window overlooked a bowling club. Then there was a very long landing leading to a box room, a bedroom and an extremely large lounge; please note 'lounge' not 'front room'! There was a good-sized front garden and the same out the back. We were allowed use of the garden and as Ted loved gardening he used to keep it looking lovely. Next to the kitchen was the bathroom and lavatory, which we had to share with the other tenants. Still, after two years on a put-you-up at Mum's and with all the arguments we used to have, this was heaven.

Susan had her own bedroom, and was already saying 'Mum, Mum'. This thrilled me, as usually a baby's first words are 'Dad, Dad'.

Now big problems – furniture required. Susan's room was lovely; my dad had decorated it. She already had a cot and Reg, with Dad's help, had made her a small wardrobe. Her cot was white, so her little wardrobe was painted white with a little teddy bear stencilled on. Yes, I was happy with her room.

But the kitchen cum living room was a horror. The sink was a browny yellow and only five inches deep with a curtain underneath stretched over two hooks and a wire. The dirt bucket (no pedal bins in those days) went behind the curtain under the sink. Dad came up and decorated the kitchen and it started to look more presentable. He was working for Express Dairies at this time, which were like cafes that sold dairy products so you could go there for coffee or tea as well as being able to do your shopping and meet friends. The Express Dairies' colour scheme was blue and white. The floor was made of blue and white tiles and Dad was given a lot of these tiles to throw away, so he threw them our way. Reg then picked out the good ones and, hey presto, we had an extremely posh floor, much better than the floorboards we had been walking on.

Reg now came up with a very good idea, or so we thought. As I mentioned before Reg was always cold, but we could not afford an electric blanket, so he thought he would make his own. The owner of the sweet shop opposite us gave Reg a large sweet tin. Inside he placed a bulb in a holder which had a long flex with a plug on the end. Then about an hour before going to bed, we plugged it in, the bulb lit up inside the tin and this contraption was placed between the sheets. We had to move it around now and then or it scorched the sheets. But it worked! We had a nice warm bed so top marks to Reg for ingenuity!

Eventually we furnished the flat alright. We went to Smart's furniture shop and on the 'never, never plan' (which meant you paid weekly) we were able to get a three-piece suite, a dining-room suite and kitchen cabinets. All this took us two years to pay off.

Reg and I had our first television set given to us by a friend who had upgraded to a better set. We were very grateful but it was so ugly! It looked like a small coffin with a nine-inch screen near the top. Still the picture was good and we were able to enjoy the programmes.

In spite of my first impressions, the Macs were lovely people. They couldn't have children but loved Susan and would babysit for us and call us up to watch their television before we had our own. To me this was a real treat, as Al was a great cook and would bring in hot sausage rolls and cakes while we were watching television.

So, at last, we had our own home, lovely neighbours and an adorable baby. It was so much nicer than being at '64' and the old put-you-up. We now lived in Chiswick High Road, with a bus stop outside the house, Marks & Spencer's a little way along the road and good old Woolworth's a little further which, in those days was everybody's favourite shop. This suited Reg and me fine, so my warmest thanks to Papa Shoot for finding our first home.

83

Although it was wonderful to have our own place, everyday life was tough in the early days. Coal was short and I had to go to the coal dump where they sold you just two bags for each person. So my routine was that after the baby's feed, I went off to get coal for the fire. I hated this as it was about a 25-minute walk then quite a queue when you got there. Luckily I had a pram with a tray underneath by the wheels where I could store the bags of coal or I don't know how I would have lugged them home. One day it was snowing and the snow kept clogging the pram wheels and it was really hard to push but I finally got home and got a fire going.

Life was hard at this time because I had had to stop work, so we only had Reg's money to live on, but then my dad bought me a sewing machine as I was good at needlework. This was a big help as I could now do home sewing. I worked for a small firm making blouses and little boys' trousers. The firm used to deliver the material already cut out and I got paid one shilling a blouse and nine pence for a pair of trousers. It certainly helped and I was at home so I could look after my baby at the same time.

Like a lot of young married couples, after about four years Reg and I had a few problems. I suppose, looking back, it was not really anyone's fault but money problems, a young baby and our different cultures and upbringing meant that I was starting to get really low, having what I called my Newbury evacuation feeling.

Because I worked at home, the only company I had was a small toddler, so I really looked forward to Reg coming home from work for some adult conversation. The trouble was that when he did get in, he would have his dinner then go straight to sleep in his chair. When he woke up he went for a pint in the working men's club opposite, so once again I was on my own. Susan would be in her bed asleep and, with no television of our own, I used to feel quite miserable. I did try to explain to Reg but he really did not understand. Finally, one morning I told him I was leaving but he took no notice and went off to work.

So I did leave him and went back to my parents. In those days if you were married you stayed married and worked it out, so my parents tried to make me go back. All to no avail; I was determined to have a better life.

I could not afford a proper moving van but I needed to move Susan's cot, pram, little wardrobe and all sorts of other bits and pieces. Opposite us there was a greengrocer who had a horse and cart, and he offered to move me for a minimal amount of money, so I arranged it with him. He came over with his horse and cart parked outside the house, then with his mate he put all the baby things and the cases with our clothes on the cart. Finally, he lifted me onto the front seat with Susan on my knee. Then much to my surprise he took the blanket off the horse and put it round Susan's and my legs. Up he got into his seat next to me and said 'You alright, duck?', and off we went with people in the street all staring at us. When we got to my mum's house, my dear old dad was waiting to unload the cart.

That evening we were settling in when there was a knock at the door. Dad went as we guessed it was Reg. Mum and I heard Reg arguing with Dad who had told him I did not want to see him. Reg finally went away, only to keep coming back time and time again. My parents said I should get legal custody of Susan, in case he took Susan away from me. This scared me so I did what they suggested and Reg received a notice to appear in court. That did it! Reg's mum came over to our house and, poor soul, she was so upset. It was the first time she had been in Mum's house and there were more arguments between them, but I was adamant I would not go back.

The day in court arrived. I was utterly miserable with a boil on my nose due to all the upset. When Dad and I arrived Reg was already there and he looked a little under the weather too. Questions were asked first of him, then me. It was horrible – all our personal life discussed in court. However, I gained custody of Susan with Reg having visiting rights. It was all over in about ten minutes.

I was with my parents for about six months. It worked well, as my mum went to work in the daytime and I worked in the evenings at the Lyons factory, packing pies from 6pm to 10pm, so someone was there all the time for Susan.

It worried me that Reg might take Susan out on his own, so when he suggested I go along for a trip to Brighton to see his aunt with them I agreed. After that, Reg came round regularly and took Susan and me out a lot. Eventually, all my old feelings returned and he talked me into going back to him. He certainly had a way with words and I fell for him all over again.

***

Over the next few years, we had some happy times watching Susan grow into a lovely girl and thrive at her primary school. Then, what a surprise! Talk about what goes around comes around: Susan's name was put forward for a scholarship at Godolphin and Latymer, the same school I had run away from! She passed her eleven-plus exam and was selected for the entrance exam. I knew the headmistress liked to interview the mothers too. I was wondering if the same headmistress was still there. Would she recognise me? Would this ruin Susan's chances of getting a place? This would be a pity because the school was the right one for her and I knew she would love it.

When we arrived a teacher took Susan away and asked me to wait by the headmistress's office. When the door opened, I heard the headmistress talking and I knew that, yes, it was the same headmistress. That set me off worrying again. I was eventually called into the office and the headmistress came towards me with a big smile and outstretched hands and said, 'Good morning. I remember you from our evacuation to Newbury.' She was so friendly and told me how the school records had been lost on the journey back home from Newbury. We then talked about Susan's previous school work and I left. She seemed impressed but you never know; we just had to wait and see. At last the wait was over. Susan had won her place and was accepted, so now just like me, off to Kinch & Lack for her uniform!

***

Susan's school used to have fêtes in the summer and the girls thought up all sorts of ideas for their stalls or events.

One year Susan dreamed up something special. She'd had several lessons at a riding school in Wimbledon and loved horses, so she thought that horse rides would be a great way to raise money for the school. First she had to get the headmistress's permission. She thought it over for a few days then called Susan into her office and gave her the go-ahead but only if the horse kept to a specific side track as she did not want the playing field spoilt. This was agreed so then Susan had to ask the riding school for a horse.

Off Susan went to the riding school in Wimbledon and, much to my surprise more than hers, they were delighted and promised to bring the horses over as they liked to see young girls interested in riding. No one at the school, apart from the head and teachers, knew anything about this; you can imagine when Susan came in with someone leading the horse the excitement and disbelief from the pupils. Susan had crowds of children all crowding round for rides and Susan led that horse up and down goodness knows how many times; she made most of the money for her school that day. I must say Reg and I were watching and felt so proud of her; then we went home and left her to it. We couldn't wait for her to come home to hear all the news about the fête and of course her horse rides. This was our first inkling that Susan was going to be someone who would make her mark on the world.

Everything was beginning to settle down: Susan was doing well at school, Reg was happy in his work and I kept on my work in the primary school as a dinner lady because I liked all the holidays. Susan had just turned twelve, when much to my surprise I became pregnant again. Reg and I were very pleased but how do you tell a twelve-year-old her mother is pregnant? In fact, Susan was fine about it and very helpful through my pregnancy. The family was astonished but my mum-in-law was over the moon.

Graham was born on 23 November 1963. I was in labour the night President John F. Kennedy was assassinated and the hospital went haywire. People were so shocked because it was unexpected and he was so young. My feelings were all upside-down as having just gone into the delivery ward my mind was all over the place.

So now we were complete: I had a boy and a girl. I was longing to see Susan and find out what she thought of her little brother. The Jewish side of the family like the birth of a boy, as it continues the family name and line but the mother is looked upon as the head and I am told this is because you are sure the mother is the true blood line.

Graham contributed to the family income from a very early age. One of Reg's relatives, Stella, thought Graham was a really beautiful child and suggested I phone an agent about him doing child modelling. Stella ran a drama and dancing school and gave me an agent's name to telephone. I popped it into my bag and thought no more of it until I got home.

Over the next few days, I thought we might as well find out what it was all about. The agent, Norrie Carr, asked to see Graham and she seemed quite impressed with his blond hair and cherubic face. He looked like an angel! She agreed to put him on her books and he had a lot of work, including shoots for Mothercare and Smith's crisps. He was very busy and he had a great time. For one advert, we had to go to Barnstable in Devon and they booked us into an expensive hotel with the crew. Graham was asked to look after the camera for the cameraman and he hung onto it with both hands and was so pleased. The crew loved him. For the advert, he had to run down a path into a cottage where a lady was using a loom, then stand and talk to her. He was only three but he acted like a real professional. We never saw this advert as it was for America but we started watching the adverts more than television programmes! We met Vanessa Redgrave when she was playing the part of Isadora Duncan and Graham was needed for a photo shoot.

Mind you, he wasn't always an angel. Once, when Reg's friend Cyril and his wife came round for supper, the men decided to get fish and chips which saved me a lot of cooking. We were all sitting round the table enjoying our fish and chips when Graham, who was playing about, went under the table. He had an old coil from one of Reg's cars and touched Cyril's leg under his trouser above his sock. Cyril yelled and jumped up, the table went sideways and all our food went flying. No one was hurt and Cyril was a good sport and chased Graham round the flat. Reg was always teaching Graham about electrics; he was a natural. It is no surprise he's an electronic expert today.

89

The time came for Graham to start school but he was getting a lot of work and I had to keep asking the school for him to have time off. This made me think, because although I ran away from school, I did know how important it was to have a good education. Susan was doing so well, and I thought it was wrong to keep taking him out of school and disrupting his studies. So I explained to his agent and took him off her books; she was a charming lady and quite understood. So at the grand age of five, after two years modelling, he could now have a normal childhood again.

Once Graham was at school, I had to think about earning money again, so I went back to being a dinner lady because I could then have the same holidays as Susan and Graham, and I was at home for the family.

***

Our nephew Lawrence was thirteen years old and having his Bar Mitzvah, to celebrate his coming of age in the Jewish faith. He had to go for lessons as this was an important time for him, so he had to learn the special hymns and prayers and be taught the meaning of his commitment to his Jewish faith.

We had a service in the synagogue in the morning and dinner in a posh London hotel in the evening. This threw both Susan and me into a spin – what should we wear? To buy evening dresses was out of the question so it was decided I would make them. This was one big headache! Susan designed her dress, white lace with a high neck, very plain 'A' line which was fashionable at the time. For me, I bought a dressmaker's pattern with a straight across neck, no sleeves and floor length, with the skirt from under the bust, flaring out in beautiful gold brocade. The dresses were gorgeous but now we had to find accessories, so off Susan and I went looking. I found some long pale lemon net gloves in a bridesmaids' shop in Hammersmith and Susan spotted some silver tights and said, 'Ooh, yes!'. I said, 'Ooh, no!', but she was determined. I must admit they went perfectly with her frock. She painted a pair of shoes silver and as I already had a pair of gold shoes, we were all set. Reg was OK, as he and his brother hired suits. Graham was only about four years old, so he could attend the ceremony but not the dinner. Without any hesitation Al stepped in and said she'd have him. So everybody ready, let's go!

The evening dresses were just for the evening so we wore ordinary smart clothes for the synagogue. We met a lot of Reg's relatives who had never met me but showed no surprise I was a Christian. The service was quite long and Lawrence said his prayers and his speeches. I cannot tell you very much as, to be truthful, I really did not understand the service, but my mum-in-law and Lawrence's parents were very pleased with him so all was well.

Once we got home and Graham was with Al upstairs, Reg, Susan and I got all dressed up in our evening gear. We arrived at the hotel and Reg's brother Geoffrey, his wife Terry, and his children Angela and Lawrence were in a line at the door of the banquet room to greet their guests. Terry was a lovely, sophisticated lady and she looked so beautiful, but I think Susan and I held our own; we looked good too and, oh yes, Susan's silver tights were the talk of the young girls – they all wanted them!

Lawrence sat at an oblong table with his immediate family and their parents. This was slightly higher than our tables which were scattered around the dining hall. I remember everyone saying how delicious the food was, and there were speeches and it was so nice for me (and especially Susan) to meet our other relatives and get a glimpse of Jewish culture.

Another happy memory was in 1997, when I was seventy. I had the biggest birthday surprise of my life. Graham was picking us up and taking us to Oxford to meet Susan and we were going out for a birthday meal. He stopped outside Lincoln College and said, 'Can you and Dad go in and tell Susan we are here? I'll wait in the car. I won't be a minute.' This seemed a little peculiar. Anyway, Reg held the door open and as I walked in there was a room full of people. I saw my brother in the corner and wondered why is he here, as he had cancer and lived in Kippax up north, next to Leeds. I ran over to him and then it dawned on me: all these people were family; it was a surprise party! Dinner was in college in a private room. We first had drinks and chatted, then went through to the adjoining room and wow! The table was shaped like a horse-shoe, with beautiful flower arrangements and cards where we were to sit: Reg and I in the middle at the bend of the table with the children either side of us. Mr Walgi (my boss in the chemist's where I worked) and his wife were there as I had been with them now for ten years and had also socialised with them. Shaneeze, his wife, looked beautiful. We had a wonderful meal, with very attentive waiters in white gloves, but there was more to come.

The lights went out and two waiters came in carrying a beautiful cake, with all the candles alight and every one sang 'Happy Birthday'. I was crying with emotion. Susan gave a wonderful speech, paying Reg and me such compliments. As a child we had never had any birthday parties but this one was the tops; it couldn't have been any better. How lucky I was!

**

The years were passing so quickly. Reg's mum had died and so had Papa Shoot. My father passed away as well. But dear old Mum was still with us, living in sheltered accommodation and in quite good health. Reg and I were doing OK, still going on our trips to Brighton. I think we were on our fourth old banger and still enjoying life.

Then in the early 1970s I hit a bad spell. I became ill, lost weight and had nasty pains in between my shoulder blades. The doctors said it was nerves, or just the 'change of life'. This went on for a year; I was so weak I could hardly stand. I never went out which was just not like me. However, one night I was so bad they rushed me to hospital and a very young doctor suggested that maybe I had an ulcer ... No, no, no they said; the pain's in the wrong place. They decided to X-ray me anyway and there it was, a lovely big duodenal ulcer! Everyone was so pleased to have at last found the problem. I had the operation and have been fine ever since.

I remember the surgeon sitting on my bed the next morning ordering me egg, bacon and sausage for breakfast and saying if you can eat that I'll let you home in a week. That breakfast was scrumptious; I did gobble it up and enjoyed every mouthful – my first real food for a year. I had lived on milk and marshmallows for so long that it was wonderful to be able to eat proper food again and I really started to appreciate the little things in life. Without the down times in life, you don't really enjoy the good times. Why is it when you are seriously ill, you think of the little things in life?

Like my Susan standing up in the back of the car with one arm round my neck and one arm round Reg's neck singing 'These are the parents'. Or Graham, about five years old, coming out of school with a flashing torch bulb taped to his nose. He had fixed a torch bulb somehow on a long wire to a battery and a switch. He fixed it to his nose, and put his hand in his pocket, turning it on and off. Or Reg giving me a cardboard Easter egg with my second engagement ring inside; this one I did like! My family, my life, my everything.

7

The End of an Era
2005–2010

After fifty-five years the time had come for us to leave our home in Chiswick and move into sheltered housing. I felt quite sad to leave the old flat, as it had been our first real home. The children had grown up there and we had so many memories. Mac had died a long time ago and eventually as Al got older she went to live with her brother. So there was no more Mac calling over the banisters, 'Night, night Dolly', and catching me in my curlers.

Their flat above ours had been empty for a few years, so it was very eerie along our landing especially at night. Also Reg had had two strokes and although he'd recovered, he was ninety and I was seventy-eight so we had to be sensible. I had been trying to persuade Reg to move to sheltered housing for a few years and he had finally given in. Graham was still living with us but was thinking of buying a bungalow. Our sheltered flat came first, so I left Graham a cupboard full of food as he would not be leaving for another two weeks. He always teased me because I forgot to leave him a tin opener.

To pack up your home after fifty-five years is horrendous, especially as we were moving to a much smaller flat, though it wasn't very far away in Brentford. What to keep, what to take – I really did not know where to start. Our new flat was ideal for us: a lounge, a bedroom, a kitchen and a super bathroom with a shower. Luckily it was newly decorated, with all new kitchen units and a completely new fitted bathroom. There was central heating with a heater in each room, so we could control how hot we wanted the flat to be. It was in a block of thirty-eight flats with a massive garden. We had a communal room where we could play bingo and have parties, and three mornings a week there was a 'coffee morning', when our warden or, to give her her formal title, 'sheltered scheme manager' (SSM), would come and join us and give us any news or tell us of any events coming up.

The SSM came round every morning to see you were OK otherwise it was just like an ordinary flat and you were left alone to do as you pleased. You did your own shopping and cooking. There was a red cord in each room to pull if you were ill and in a short time a voice would talk to you and get either the doctor or ambulance. For our age, this was ideal.

Graham was so good when we were packing up and helped as much as he could. Susan had given us a beautiful two-sofa lounge set with footstool to match which had a corner piece to join the two sofas together; it looked so nice in our new home. Graham gave us a gorgeous mirror, with a gold frame with a picture of swans carved in the corner. What with white sofas and the mirror above we were beginning to look quite posh.

The move itself was handled by Graham and his friend Dave, who'd said to us, 'I'll move you – don't pay all that money for a removals firm'. He had a large open-top trailer which he could attach to his car. So he and Graham made goodness knows how many journeys from Chiswick to Brentford. It must have been hard work but they made light of it. The funniest thing was seeing my wardrobe on top of Dave's trailer – good job we had no beds to move. We bought new beds which had already been delivered. At the end of the day everything was in place; Dave and Graham sat down and had a beer, exhausted but laughing about the mishaps they had had on the way. The Greenfields had arrived at Lambert Lodge!

So although nostalgic for the old days, Reg and I were all nice and cosy in our own self-contained modern flat. It was like being married all over again! There was plenty going on if you wished to join in. When we first came here we used to go down for most things just to be sociable. Our SSM, and Judith, who is the daughter of one of the other tenants Ada, used to bring in cakes and hot sausage rolls for the bingo players and we'd have a really fun time.

We had been there about a year when I suggested to the SSM that I'd like a party to celebrate my seventy-ninth birthday. The food came from Marks & Spencer and my daughter Susan bought all the drink. It really was such a mixed crowd and of all ages from little children to my friends in Lambert Lodge. Sixty-four people altogether! We started about 3 o'clock and we were still dancing right through until 10–11pm. It was to say thank you as well, to everyone at Lambert Lodge for the help they gave us when we moved in.

Reg and I were very happy in our new home, but unfortunately after a couple of years we had to stop going to bingo and some of the other functions as Reg couldn't hear too well and got very tired. Mind you, even at ninety-five he was still on the ball and ready for a joke. We still had a laugh about him winning the knobbly knees competition at Eastbourne and the time when Graham was in a boat on a boating lake, and took a step to get in the boat, but somehow it moved and he took a step into the water and was soaked right up to his waist.

We also used to talk about the time when we thought Reg would drown. It gave me a real shock. Reg couldn't swim, but he was in the sea having fun in an inner tube from a car tyre, and got caught in a wave which kept throwing him up and back on the breakwaters. His spectacles were washed away but he finally managed to free himself and we looked down and his glasses had washed up onto my ankles. This certainly was a miracle. Since this happened it has made me wonder if there is someone, somewhere out there, looking after us.

Although Reg couldn't do too much once he got to ninety-five, we used to love to reminisce about the happy times we had had and how Susan and Graham, our wonderful children, would always include us in their celebrations.

Susan and Graham are very private people and hate it when I rattle on about their achievements, so I do not mean to go on about how clever they are, but I have to tell you a couple of things or you will never know some of the special times Reg and I enjoyed.

For a few years, Susan was Director of the Royal Institution (RI) where Faraday did his experiments, so she often met the Queen and Duke of Edinburgh when they came to visit. She also became a baroness in her own right and so gave speeches in the House of Lords. I must tell you how I met the Queen and Duke of Edinburgh. The RI had had a face lift and the Queen and the Duke of Edinburgh were coming to view, so the Queen could unveil a plaque. This meant that each department of the

RI would have representatives in a line and the Queen would meet them and shake their hand and they would curtsey or bow as the case may be. So you can imagine how Reg and I felt when we were told *we* would be in one of the line-ups. We arrived in Graham's Audi; gosh my son looked so smart! We were met by Susan at the door and then when the Queen and Duke arrived we were all ready in position. Suddenly there was a hush, with people whispering 'The Queen's coming, the Queen's coming', and there she was in the doorway! I was first in line and Susan said 'This is my mum'. I had a feeling I had never had before shaking hands with the Queen. She had such beautiful eyes and a lovely smile. My dad would have been so proud!

I curtsied as best I could, because my knee was hurting. Then the Queen was shaking Reg's hand and going along the line. Later on the Duke of Edinburgh had a long chat with Reg and me, and asked about Graham and where he was. I pointed Graham out and the Duke went over to him and they started laughing and talking. This was truly a most wonderful experience.

We also went to a garden party at Buckingham Palace; this was delightful and so unexpected, but Susan had an invitation and could take two guests, so Reg and I were once more going into a different world. I was not on Dad's barrow dreaming but in a Rolls-Royce. The gardens were so beautiful and I had cucumber sandwiches. There were so many important people and celebrities it was hard not to stare. The Queen was coming so we made two lines and she walked along talking to people with her attendants behind her. When she came to the end she went into a marquee where her friends and family were to have tea.

All good things come to an end but to round the day off we were meeting Graham at the Ritz for dinner. I felt I was in a dream and had come such a long way, from creeping down the school playing field with my carrier bag and jam sandwiches to dining at the Ritz!

***

As Reg and I got older, birthdays became very special, and we would celebrate at Susan's house in Oxford, with family and friends. When it came to Reg's ninetieth birthday the children asked their Dad what he would like as a present. There was no hesitation – a flying lesson! We all looked at him in amazement. However, a flying lesson was booked for him and off we went to the airport just outside Oxford. Reg was so excited and told me that he would wiggle the wings as he came in to land. We walked with Reg as far as we were allowed, cameras at the ready and off he flew. My guess is he felt good because at last he could fly a plane. He had tried to get into the Royal Air Force during the war, but his eyesight was not good enough. He was up for about half hour and then we spotted him flying back, and yes, he wiggled the plane's wings. Well done, Reg, at ninety years old! Afterwards he laughed saying that getting in and out of the plane was harder than flying it.

Over the years we had both had some health problems: Reg had had a couple of strokes and throat trouble, and I've had two new knees and a nasty ulcer. I won't talk about this as it's too depressing but we had both come through OK and still had our brains working. We had worked out a super routine. Both of us liked a little gamble: Reg was into roulette and I like the horses. Our bookie knew us now and after we'd laid our bets he kindly kept an eye on Reg, giving him cups of tea and biscuits, while I went to do a bit of shopping. I was usually away about forty-five minutes, then I'd come back and home we'd go. Sometimes we lost, sometimes we won, but we were still in the outside world and meeting people and really that is all that matters.

Another highlight in our later years was when Reg and I were invited to Herriot-Watt University in Edinburgh. Our daughter Susan was going to be made Chancellor of the university and we were offered a flight to Edinburgh, two nights in a hotel, a car with a driver to show us around Edinburgh, and an invitation to Susan's installation ceremony and dinner. I have always been frightened of flying but this was so important to me that I knew we had to go.

As it was an early flight, we stayed overnight in a hotel near Heathrow Airport. The next morning we were picked up and taken to the airport. We were so pleased to see Susan, who calmed my nerves, but Reg wasn't nervous at all; he was too excited at the prospect of being on a plane.

We had coffee and watched the planes come and go through the lounge window until our flight was called. Now my tummy was turning over. Susan had our boarding ticket and we were able to have a front seat with plenty of leg room. I heard the engine start up, and clung to the arms of my seat waiting to be up in the air but felt nothing. Reg turned to me and called, 'Look! We're up!' I couldn't believe it; I hadn't felt anything. My tummy settled and I leaned over Susan to look out the window but all I could see were clouds, like cotton wool. The flight was short but once again I worried about coming down. Susan had explained it might make my ears pop. We had a little bump as the wheels touched the ground but everything was so smooth; why on earth had I got so worked up? In fact, between you and me, I felt flying was a piece of cake!

Susan was busy at the university the next morning and the car came to take us around Edinburgh. The first thing I asked for was to see the theatre and the digs where I stayed as a dancer in the war. Now it was me who was excited. We had such a lovely time in that car just driving around. The time passed so quickly, and then we were dropped off at the university.

Susan was being photographed in her academic gown – my, she looked so important. The photographer asked if we'd like a photo with her. They didn't have to ask twice! This photo is hanging on the wall in my lounge now, and I feel so proud. Susan delivered a fantastic speech and received a standing ovation. I was tapped on the shoulder by a lady behind where I was sitting. 'Isn't she wonderful?' she said. She never knew I was her mum and I never told her.

I enjoyed the flight home and could not believe that I had been so scared before. The whole trip was marvellous, especially seeing Susan get such a warm reception. I never thought how happy I could be, and it was very kind of the university to give Reg and me such a perfect day.

***

Then came what was probably the best birthday celebration ever, my eightieth. I never thought my seventieth party could be beaten but this time Susan told me where the party was to be. Guess where? The House of Lords! My dad would have been so proud. Dad loved the royal family and our British heritage. As a child he had taken me to see the Houses of Parliament and Big Ben and we always watched the changing of the guard. Now I was going to be entertained inside the House of Lords! Once again my emotions got to me and the tears had to be fought back. The taxi was on time and off we went, all dressed up but this time we did have somewhere to go! The Houses of Parliament loomed up and

101

suddenly I felt nervous but, on arrival, people were kissing and cuddling me and the presents were piling up on the table, photos were being taken and waiters coming round with drinks and canapés. Then it was time for dinner. We were all ushered into the dining room and that was when I saw my magnificent cake. Dinner was fantastic as were the speeches afterwards. Yes, I did give a speech which I had written at home and planned to give without my notes, but I was so overtaken with emotion I had to read it out. At the end, Graham took my arm and we all went off home. My most wonderful birthday was over but as I waved Graham off in his car, I was overcome and said to Reg, 'We must have done something right'. He nodded and gave me a little kiss. Perfect!

8

'Till Death Do Us Part'
2011–2012

It was a cold day, so I mentioned to Reg that maybe he should stay in and not come shopping with me. 'Definitely not!' was his answer. 'I have a new roulette system I want to try out.' That was Reg: if he had a new system no way could I deter him, so off we went. Amazingly he was ready before me and he was eager to get going.

We saw the bus coming so I called to Reg not to hurry as I'd stop it, which I did. I turned round for Reg and he was not there. He had fallen off the curb sideways into the road and of course the bus was blocking him from my sight. The bus driver saw him and jumped off the bus and tried to pick him up but it was no use. Another two men came off the bus and together we got him onto his feet and on the pavement but he was shouting in agony and could not put his foot to the ground.

There was a small paper shop nearby and we managed to get him there and they kindly fetched him a chair. The bus driver was concerned but obviously had to go. Once in the shop I dialled 999 and the ambulance came in about fifteen minutes. Poor Reg had broken his hip and was clinging onto my hand and would not let go. They were going to keep him in hospital for an operation. Although he was in a lot of pain he was not happy about staying in hospital.

I phoned Graham as he was nearest to me and had a car, and he came over straight away and phoned Susan to let her know. We stayed with Reg for as long as we were allowed, then Graham brought me home. After his operation we were all there. Susan had come from Oxford and Graham had collected me. Reg was happy with all the attention he was getting and the three of us all sat round his bed chatting. Susan, being allied to the medical profession, went and had a chat with his doctor, then came and told us how he was, in a way we could understand. He didn't seem too bad but we had to remember he was ninety-five years old.

The children were so good. Susan was up and down from Oxford and Graham was collecting me every day. After about three days his breathing became very bad and he had to have an oxygen mask on; he hated this and kept pulling it off. In fact he broke four of them, so in the end they put gloves on him. These were like boxing gloves, but of a soft white material. I think this was the last straw for my poor Reg; he couldn't talk to us because of the mask and he was so distressed.

Susan and Graham tried to point to letters of the alphabet to spell out things but he was just too weary to bother. He just seemed to fade away. The doctors said his organs had failed one by one. He was moved to a side ward and we knew we were going to lose him. His family came but he was not conscious; however, it was good to see them and they all stayed quite a while.

Of course he left us, and after being together for sixty-three years it was as if I had lost a part of me; my friend, my husband, the father of my children and my lover. I felt utterly wretched. Thank goodness I had two lovely children who I knew with all my heart cared about me and understood my grief.

Although Reg died in 2011, I am finding it very hard to write this as memories of the funeral come flooding back. It was a nasty, gloomy day and the rain poured down. I was so pleased when Susan and Graham arrived early; without my dear children I would have been lost.

Although he was eighty-five years old, my brother Fred travelled all the way from Bournemouth; Reg and he had been such good pals, there was no way he would not come and say goodbye to Reg himself. Sadly my other brother John had already died.

This was no ordinary funeral as Reg was Jewish, so how could we arrange things so everybody was alright and no one upset? We knew he wanted to be cremated at Mortlake Crematorium as we had discussed this and he said to me it was because he knew that's what I wanted for myself and he wanted us to be together. So I suggested to the children that a rabbi say prayers instead of a priest but still at Mortlake Crematorium. The funeral parlour that was dealing with his funeral phoned the crematorium and they agreed.

Now this was fine, but could we find a rabbi who would help us? Susan knew who to ask and we were lucky she found a rabbi who would conduct the service. The crematorium was so full some people had to stand. There were very few flowers as in the Jewish religion you are not allowed to send flowers. But the children and I sent wreaths; I couldn't let Reg go without them. The Jewish people understood and were alright about it.

When the coffin came in, it was so hard to hold the tears back but my children held my hands and Fred had his arm around my shoulder. Susan gave a marvellous tribute to her dad, then two very dear friends, Carolyn and Shahin, each gave a beautiful reading. We then all sang 'our song', 'Over the Rainbow', which was so touching. Two special friends, Professor John Stein and Professor Clive Coen, both gave tributes. Had Reg been alive he would have loved it because they spoke so well of him. Reg's nephew Lawrence gave a Jewish prayer, which was called Kaddish, in Hebrew. The rabbi had been saying prayers through-out the service. I was alright until the curtains closed around the coffin, and then I cried.

After the service we went on to celebrate his life in the ban-quet hall at the local Holiday Inn with a beautiful meal. His cousin Susan Soloman lit the candle, which in Reg's religion has to burn for a few days. This time all the Jewish people and the Christian people mingled and were so friendly it was good to see, not like our wedding where they sat opposite each other!

After the celebration of Reg's life was over, my wonderful son slept on my sofa so I wouldn't be alone. I knew I had to adjust eventually but it was difficult as we did everything together. I had known Reg since I was fourteen years old. I was lucky to have such a charming, caring husband. He is still sadly missed by all of us and the rabbi has phoned me several times to see if I'm alright. Also Reg's relatives still keep in touch. Life is different now but with the help of my children I will cope.

9

New Beginnings: Dancing Again
2012–

After Reg's funeral, it took me a quite a while to get used to being alone. Having been married for sixty-three years, life was very strange now. I was so happy we made the decision to move to Lambert Lodge and I've made a lot of friends there, who helped me in so many ways. Even with these kind people around, I still felt lonely and missed Reg so much.

So a plan was needed. First, keep in touch with the outside world and go out every day, anywhere, even a bus ride. Second, Sudoku is good as it keeps the brain busy but it's not very entertaining. So third, go to the Albany Centre run by Age Concern and see what they have to help keep me entertained. I looked at everything they had to offer on a weekly basis and, wait a minute, what is that? Line dancing! I could do that I was sure, although I was nearly eighty-four. I was determined to try. My dancing days were not over yet!

My plan worked well. I went through to the little restaurant just off the large room where the dancing would be held to have a cup of tea. When I entered there was a group of ladies laughing and talking. I asked one lady about line dancing, and apparently they all attended the lesson and said it was really good, but I would have to speak to Rosemary, the dance teacher. As they talked to me, my nerves began to settle. I hadn't danced (except ballroom dancing) for more than sixty years, so I hoped I wasn't going to make a fool of myself. Anyway I was determined to have a go.

Rosemary walked in; a tall, sophisticated lady, smart and elegant, she was so charming and put me at my ease by saying, 'If you know your left from your right and keep up with the music, you will be able to line dance'. This really impressed me and took all my fears away. I've been with Rosemary's girls now for almost a year and can honestly say Monday is my favourite day. I feel like I'm young again, as I'm doing what I love, dancing. This is something I can look forward to and when you are getting on in years this is what you need. Something that will get you out and something you really, really do enjoy.

After line dancing some of us go into the little restaurant where they make the most fabulous fish and chips. I'm back where I belong. I did say what goes around comes around. Roll on Mondays!

**

When Reg died, the children thought a computer would be an asset to me. I know the computer is a marvellous invention so we went off to PC World. This was my son Graham's field, so he pointed one out and discussed it with Susan but all I was bothered about was having a white printer so it all matched the room it was going in. Susan said I needed a mouse, printing paper and a case for the laptop.

Graham came over to my flat, set it all up, arranged access to the internet and sorted out insurance. He promised to come back in a couple of days to show me how to use it. I was longing to switch it on but I dared not. Well, the big day came and Graham made me sit by the computer as he sat alongside me and gave me a short lesson. Then he said I would learn best by trial and error, and off he went. I am not stupid but it seemed to be very complex. I did try Graham's 'trial and error' method, but it didn't work!

So the next day, I bought a book for the over-sixties (though I really wanted one for the over eighties). It was called *Computers Made Easy*. Easy? They didn't know the meaning of the word easy. If that is easy, I hate to think what difficult would mean. Not to be outdone, I went back to Age Concern and yes I was in luck, they had IT lessons! They were run by voluntary students. My first lesson was on Word, so I could get used to the mouse and keyboard. Ah, the mouse! Why does my cursor go everywhere except where I want it?

I had a few lessons and my neighbour Sheena also helped me out. If our SSM had time, she would pop up too and help me. Finally, I got the hang of sending emails, or so I thought! But either they didn't arrive or went to the wrong person. Eventually I started getting better but then suddenly adverts kept popping up just as I was sending an email. This frustrated me; I couldn't find my cross at the top as that had disappeared so I did that dreaded thing and switched the whole computer off at the main plug.

The next day I switched my computer back on again, thinking all would be normal but no, a message stated I had switched it off in the wrong way. I could see this computer was having none of me and my bad behaviour. Graham sorted it out on his next visit, gave me a lesson and explained a lot more to me. Now one year later, I can Google, use Word, send emails and open an attachment. Oh dear, there is so much more to learn but I will conquer this computer!

***

Walking home the other day it suddenly seemed quiet in the side streets. It made me think how different things are today. Where is our favourite Bobby the friendly policeman? Or the rag and bone man calling out, 'Any old rags?' Even the newspaper man on his stall would be calling out 'Get your newspaper' and repeating what was in the headlines. Where are the children playing in the street? How sad for them, their parents too frightened to let them out. We had a park keeper and friendly neighbours who'd keep an eye out, so it was safe for us to play in the park or street all day long.

Where has all the glamour gone? The girls today are all in the same jeans, straight hair and T-shirt – is it laziness? Even when the war was on with bombs dropping, the girls always made sure they looked good for the Saturday night dance. We couldn't get stockings so we painted our legs and drew a line up the back of the leg for the seam. We wouldn't let Hitler take our glamour away. When you had a perm you were wired up to a machine and although you knew the siren could go you still chanced it. Many a time, me included, ladies came running out of the hairdressers with curlers in their hair.

The war was the time of the big bands. I remember Billy Cotton's band, and it was wonderful. People would chat to each other on the buses, but now no one talks; they have their earphones on listening to music or are texting on their mobiles.

Not long ago I went to an old-time musical show with my brother Fred and that brought back some happy memories. It's a pity the London shows are so expensive; gone are the days when it was three pennies to go in the gods.

As a child, Dad and I would queue up outside the Chiswick or Shepherd's Bush Empire to sit in the gods to see the shows. The seats were really cheap because they were more like deep stairs and you didn't have to book, so as soon as the doors opened it was a mad rush to get to the front. One day Miss Merlwyn took me to the Chiswick Empire in the second row of the stalls, as she wanted me to pick up on a couple of tap steps. There I was in my best dress, hair curled, and we arrived by car. As Mum would say I felt 'really posh'.

While I was in Bournemouth recently, on holiday with my brother, we went to the theatre to see the show *Grease* and I felt so weird. This was the theatre where we had played *No, No Nanette* during the war! It brought back so many memories. When our performance was over after the show we used to go for midnight walks along the sea front, where the old barrage balloon would be flapping about in the air; planes were coming over, search-lights flashing across the sky and there was the sound of guns in the distance. Most of the men would be in uniform and of course we had the Americans. As we walked along they would greet you with a wink and smile. Oh, yes, things were very different then!

After nearly two years of being on my own, I still miss Reg but I am slowly getting used to standing on my own two feet. The things I find hard are eating in a restaurant alone, having no one to show something I might have bought and having no one to share the excitement if I have a win on my horses. It is the little things like these. And, of course, I have no one to moan to!

However, there are still so many things to look forward to, and best of all, our line-dancing troupe is giving a public performance. I'm back dancing in front of an audience again!

Life after eighty-five is OK, if you keep taking the tablets.

Epilogue

I have enjoyed chatting to you and wandering through the past. I've had my challenges to overcome: a nice girl would not go on the stage, a sensible girl would not marry outside her religion, and at the time these things were important to society, but as Frank Sinatra sang, 'I did it my way'.

What the future holds who knows, but I have enjoyed my life. I have had a lovely family, wonderful friends and a caring husband although I miss him so much. So, I think I have been very lucky and life can still go on after eighty-five if you keep looking for a challenge.

Oh, just one more thing. I do hope if there is an 'afterlife' they will have dancing up there. If not I am coming back down, finding a theatre and joining on the end of the chorus girls' line. After all no one would know. Would they?

1. Dorice as a young ballerina

2. 1932 – Dorice dancing

3. 1938 – Dorice at Miss Merlwyn's

4. Brothers John and Fred

5. Freda and Dorice

6. 1945 – Chorus line for *The Sherman Fisher Girls. Dorice is second from the right*

7. 1947 – *Dorice and Reg on their wedding day*

8. 1952 – Dorice's parents, Dorice and baby Susan

*9. 1965 – Reg with Susan and Dorice in the
dresses they made themselves*

10. *Dorice with brothers John and Fred*

11. *Dorice meeting the Queen*

12. Reg's flying lesson for his 90th birthday

13. Dorice with a Wall's ice cream cart

14. Reg and Dorice's first party in sheltered accommodation

15. 2015 — Dorice with children, Graham and Susan

A NOTE ON THE AUTHOR

Dorice Greenfield was born in 1927 on the family sofa in Acton, London, to a poor but loving family. She started dancing from a young age in order to overcome her shyness. With the breakout of the Second World War in 1939, Dorice was evacuated to the countryside, far from her family and her dancing, until she ran away from school, returning to London to begin her professional dancing career.

Dorice married a Jewish man in 1947, to the disdain of her family and society, but they stayed together for 63 years until his death in 2012, aged 95.

Dorice still lives in West London, and goes line dancing twice a week.